MILLER'S

WRIST-WATCHES

HOW TO COMPARE & VALUE

MILLER'S

WRIST-WATCHES

HOW TO COMPARE & VALUE

JONATHAN SCATCHARD CONSULTANT

Miller's Wristwatches – How to Compare & Value

Consultant Jonathan Scatchard

Principal Contributor Oliver Saunders
Contributor James Gurney

First published in Great Britain in 2004 by Miller's,
a division of Mitchell Beazley,
imprints of Octopus Publishing Group Ltd,
2–4 Heron Quays, London, E14 4JP
Reprinted 2005

Miller's is a registered trademark of Octopus Publishing Group Ltd

Senior Executive Editor	Anna Sanderson
Executive Art Editor	Rhonda Fisher
Senior Editor	Emily Anderson
Page Design	Gillian Andrews
Editor	Claire Musters
Jacket Design	Victoria Bevan
Proofreader	Miranda Stonor
Indexer	Sue Farr
Production	Sarah Rogers
Picture Research	Emma O'Neill

The publishers will be grateful for any information that will assist them in keeping future editions up to date.
While every care has been taken in the preparation of this book, neither the author nor the publisher can accept any liability for any consequence arising from the use thereof, or the information contained therein.

Values should be used as a guide only, as prices vary according to geographical location and demand. US prices have been calculated at a rate of 1.5 dollars to the pound.

ISBN 1 84000 715 X

A CIP record for this book is available from the British Library

Set in Palatino, Helvetica, and Scala Sans
Produced by Toppan Printing Co., (HK) Ltd.
Printed and bound in China

Contents

Introduction to
Wristwatches

How to Use This Book

The unique compare-and-contrast format that is the hallmark of the *Miller's How to Compare and Value* series has been specially designed to help you to identify authentic wristwatches on the market and assess their value. At the heart of this book is a series of two-page comparison spreads – 48 in all. On each spread two examples of wristwatches are pictured side-by-side and carefully analyzed to determine not only the market value of each piece, but why one is more valuable than the other.

In the comparison section you will be able to consider the context in which the watches were created, their intended uses and relative condition, and their importance in today's market. By comparing and analyzing a wide variety of items,you will gain the knowledge and skills needed to find and evaluate wristwatches and assess their worth with confidence. The illustrations and annotations, below and opposite, show how the various elements on a typical two-page comparison spread work.

The book's introductory chapters offer an overview of the wristwatches market and practical pointers on the care and display of your acquisitions. A fascinating history on the creation and development of wristwatches in Europe and the USA is illustrated with a superb array of examples.

Finally, at the back you will find information on where to see and buy wristwatches in the UK, Europe, and the USA, other sources that may advance your knowledge and understanding, and a detailed glossary.

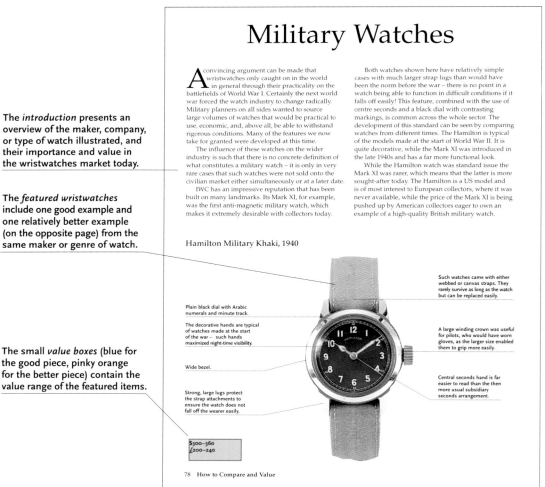

Military Watches

A convincing argument can be made that wristwatches only caught on in the world in general through their practicality on the battlefields of World War I. Certainly the next world war forced the watch industry to change radically. Military planners on all sides wanted to source large volumes of watches that would be practical to use, economic, and, above all, be able to withstand rigorous conditions. Many of the features we now take for granted were developed at this time.

The influence of these watches on the wider industry is such that there is no concrete definition of what constitutes a military watch – it is only in very rare cases that such watches were not sold onto the civilian market either simultaneously or at a later date.

IWC has an impressive reputation that has been built on many landmarks. Its Mark XI, for example, was the first anti-magnetic military watch, which makes it extremely desirable with collectors today.

Both watches shown here have relatively simple cases with much larger strap lugs than would have been the norm before the war – there is no point in a watch being able to function in difficult conditions if it falls off easily! This feature, combined with the use of centre seconds and a black dial with contrasting markings, is common across the whole sector. The development of this standard can be seen by comparing watches from different times. The Hamilton is typical of the models made at the start of World War II. It is quite decorative, while the Mark XI was introduced in the late 1940s and has a far more functional look.

While the Hamilton watch was standard issue the Mark XI was rarer, which means that the latter is more sought-after today. The Hamilton is a US model and is of most interest to European collectors, where it was never available, while the price of the Mark XI is being pushed up by American collectors eager to own an example of a high-quality British military watch.

Hamilton Military Khaki, 1940

Such watches came with either webbed or canvas straps. They rarely survive as long as the watch but can be replaced easily.

Plain black dial with Arabic numerals and minute track.

The decorative hands are typical of watches made at the start of the war – such hands maximized night-time visibility.

Wide bezel.

Strong, large lugs protect the strap attachments to ensure the watch does not fall off the wearer easily.

A large winding crown was useful for pilots, who would have worn gloves, as the larger size enabled them to grip them more easily.

Central seconds hand is far easier to read than the then more usual subsidiary seconds arrangement.

$300–360
£200–240

The *introduction* presents an overview of the maker, company, or type of watch illustrated, and their importance and value in the wristwatches market today.

The *featured wristwatches* include one good example and one relatively better example (on the opposite page) from the same maker or genre of watch.

The small *value boxes* (blue for the good piece, pinky orange for the better piece) contain the value range of the featured items.

78   How to Compare and Value

The *headline* is a brief descriptive title for each featured piece, followed by an approximate date.

The *annotations* highlight each example's "value features" – key factors such as design, technique, condition, and provenance that account for a wristwatch's relative market value.

IWC Mark XI, 1948

Mineral glass pressure-fitted under the bezel.

Large bezel has a matt finish.

The black dial contrasts well with the luminous hands, creating an instantly legible but unobtrusive watch design.

The British government arrow on the dial makes this watch extremely sought-after.

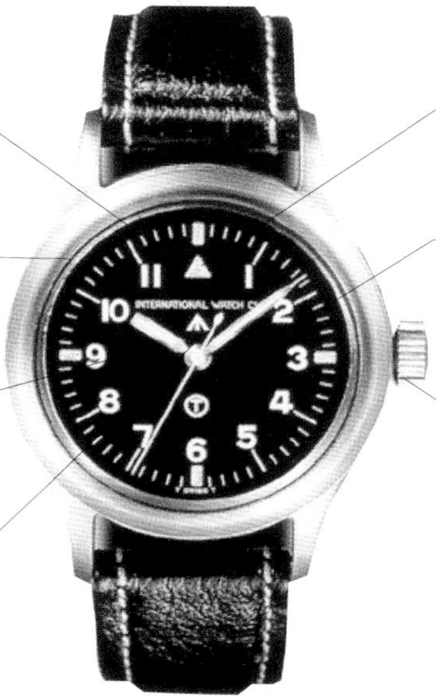

Luminous triangle and quarter bars further aid legibility.

IWC watches were among the first to incorporate central seconds hands on their watches.

Large winding crown made it easier to use the "hacking" device. (When the crown was pulled out one notch it stopped the watch, which enabled the wearer to synchronize their watch with others.)

$2,250–3,000
£1,500–2,000

- *From a collector's point of view the most desirable military watches are those that have a real provenance in the form, for example, of the British government arrow, as is found on the dial of the IWC Mark XI shown above.*
- *Always look for government procurement marks or numbers; nearly all true military watches will have one or the other.*
- *Military watches are sometimes customized to meet government specifications – for example, there are several white dial IWC Mark XIs that were modified by the UK Ministry of Defence. Such items are very rare, and are therefore worth a premium.*

IWC's Anti-magnetic Watches

IWC was one of the first companies to produce anti-magnetic movements and watches. This was in response to the increasing frequency of situations where high magnetic fields were encountered – particularly in military and industrial life. Whereas the earth's magnetic field produces a background of about 80 a/m (ampere meters), large electric engines can develop fields of tens of thousands a/m. By comparison, a non-protected watch will run erratically in fields of a few thousand a/m.

During the 1920s the German state railways requested that IWC develop a watch that was able to resist the strong fields generated by electric train engines. The result was the anti-magnetic Calibre 56 Lépine, which incorporated anti-magnetic materials for the escapement and balance assembly.

The emerging aviation industry was also demanding watches that would be able to remain reliable while being exposed for long periods to magnetic fields. The next development pioneered by IWC was the installation of a soft-iron cage around the movement. This effectively conducted magnetic fields around the movement leaving the escapement free of interference. This neat solution was included in the design of many of the pilots' watches over the years.

Military Watches 79

The *bulleted points* offer further specific information about a watchmaker or about a certain type of wristwatch.

The *feature box* provides further information on the history and development of the featured maker or genre. There is sometimes also additional information that relates to the wristwatches market or to specific production techniques.

Understanding the Market

It seems almost strange that in an era with quartz watches, which provide accurate time on a full-time basis and are available at such a low cost, people should collect mechanical wristwatches. After all, these are subject to some gain or loss in their timekeeping and are much more expensive. However, the idea of possessing something that is in part created by hand, and is made up of many moving parts, appeals to a collector as it is an expression of craftsmanship.

So who collects wristwatches? It is actually very much a male preserve. In fact, some sales of cars are themed to include sporting chronographs, such as those held annually by Bonhams in Gstaad, Monte Carlo, and Goodwood. Such wristwatches are seen to be status symbols and many who collect them will in fact wear them on appropriate occasions. For example, a Patek Philippe or Cartier gold watch on a strap – crocodile, of course – works well on a formal evening occasion. Association with events and famous people, whether film stars, sportsmen, or fictional and celluloid heroes, such as James Bond, can also attract collectors to certain models. A variation of the Navitimer, for example, was worn by Scott Carpenter on his Aurora-7 space capsule mission in May 1962.

How should the collector, whether novice or established, ideally approach the subject? In furnishing a house with antiques you would expect to acquire pieces from differing periods, countries, and values; this approach can also work in other collecting disciplines. However, it is not one that should be used in the collecting of watches. This is because there is a danger that with so many different watch manufacturers and countries of origin collectors can spread their nets too wide and end up with collections that have only a few good pieces and are rather over-balanced with watches of similar character and of no great importance or value. It is far more worthwhile and exciting to pursue watches by a particular maker, or even a particular model or generic type, and, as you will discover, this can prove to be financially rewarding too. What follows is a brief outline of the main types of watches that have collecting appeal.

▶ The connection between Omega and James Bond is well established. This particular example was bought for, and worn by, Pierce Brosnan in the 1999 Bond film *The World Is Not Enough*. The fact that it is the actual watch worn by the actor raises its value, and it was sold at Christie's in South Kensington in their annual Film and Television Memorabilia Auction for $17,625 (£11,750) in December 2001. An identical watch by Omega without the film connection would cost $1,650 (£1,100).

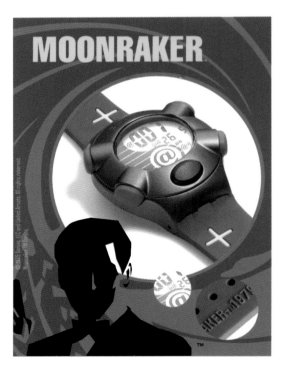

▶ Poster for the Swatch Moonraker watch, produced to commemorate James Bond's 40th anniversary in 2002. Each watch is printed with the "007" logo. This watch is an example of a trend to produce items specifically for the collectable market. Whether their value will increase, only time will tell.

Military Watches

Such watches are pieces of history as they were issued to servicemen during the various conflicts of the 20th century. They can range from the grille-covered watches produced by Omega for servicemen in World War I to the Hamilton watches produced in the USA for their Navy in World War II. The backs of such watches often have numbers or marks that identify for whom they were made. For example, the British Ministry of Defence mark is an arrow and it is found on watches made for the British armed forces during and after World War II.

Many of the watches were made by large Swiss and American watch companies such as IWC, Longines, and Hamilton. However, in the United Kingdom do not be surprised to find post-World War II examples with the name Smiths on the dial, even though this is a firm that is more usually associated with clocks.

While many military watches will sell in auction for less than $1,500 (£1,000) the more unusual examples

can command high figures. One example, auctioned at Christie's in London in June 2002, was a Rolex Submariner c.1970. This sold for $13,500 (£9,000) against a pre-sale estimate of $4,500–6,000 (£3,000–4,000). The reason for this was that it was one of a limited number of Submariners that were commissioned by the British Government in 1969 with special configurations for use by frogmen of the Royal Navy. It also had a numbered case. Although similar watches were supplied to the British Armed Forces it was this "special edition" that collectors desired.

There are examples of military watches from many countries, including the Hanhart, used by German military and navigators during World War II, and the Auricoste, which was used by French military personnel in the 1950s. These appeal not only to collectors from the respective countries but also to those who have interests in one particular period of conflict.

◀ This Czech pilot's watch, c.1920, was made by the Swiss company Longines, which is indicated on the dial. It also has the imprint of the Czech airforce on the back. Such steel watches were mass-produced for the military but because this example is in such mint condition it does suggest that it was never issued. Early watches like this are highly sought after and this example's condition gives it a high value – $525–1,650 (£350–1,100).

◀ Omega 339MU
This is a very rare pre-World War II example. It has an extra-long winding crown tomake it possible to wind the watch while wearing heavy gloves possible. This example is worth $2,250–3,000 (£1,500–2,000) today.

◀ Hamilton supplied the US army from 1943, as well as providing watches for airmen and, towards the end of World War II, for British forces. This particular example has a 24-hour dial. *See* page 78 for further details of Hamilton's military watches.

▶ This chronograph was supplied by Heuer to the German government for military use in the 1960s. It has an unidirectional bezel and the watch is very clear and easy to read. Made by one of the most desirable chronograph manufacturers it is worth $1,125–2,250 (£750–1,500).

Aviators' and Sports Watches

The chronograph, with its stopwatch function for short-interval timing (*see* page 68), has long been a favourite with collectors, and those with split-second mechanisms and minute-repeaters are especially prized. However, it should be remembered that they may be converted from pocket watches, which decreases the value.

For those interested in aviation the Angle Horaire (Hour-Angle), designed by and originally made for, Charles Lindbergh, may well appeal. Many of the watches and chronographs that were made for aviators are larger than normal wristwatches since they were designed to be worn over a flying jacket – some were even designed to be strapped to the leg.

For automobile enthusiasts, watches with curved edges were designed in the 1930s to sit on the side of the wrist to enable the driver to read the time without moving his/her hand from the steering wheel. Some chronographs were fitted with an outer tachometer ring which would allow the driver to ascertain his speed over a fixed distance on a race track. Other types of watch with motoring motifs include those made in the shape of a radiator grille (a 1940s Mido example could cost from $1,800 (£1,200) upwards depending on condition), or those given as gifts or promotional material by automobile manufacturers.

Classic Watches

Firms such as Patek Philippe, Audemars Piguet, IWC, and Vacheron & Constantin are examples of the top Swiss manufacturers and, as such, are seen as producers of classic watches. Patek Philippe is considered by many to be the Rolls-Royce of the watch world, and therefore their watches hold their popularity and their value. Rolex come a close second, especially with their Oyster model. Many collectors, mainly those who buy watches to wear, go for classic watches such as IWC's Da Vinci and Portugieser models and Audemars Piguet's Royal Oak. Some manufacturers have put early models back into production to meet the demand. For example, the Reverso, first manufactured by Jaeger-LeCoultre in 1931, is now being made again, as is Zenith's El Primero. Prices will vary depending upon where you purchase them, but watches from the 1950s and 1960s are particularly collectable in today's market.

Good design, unusual movements, and complicated mechanisms are all popular. The pinnacle of movements is the perpetual calendar, which adjusts automatically to take into account the number of days in each month and when there is a leap year.

Classic watches in mint condition will probably be bought to go in a collection rather than be worn, since a knock during wear would reduce the value a great deal.

▼ This 1960s Seafarer chronograph by Heuer bears the name of the well-known travel specialist it was made for – Abercrombie & Fitch. It has both 30-minute and 12-hour counters and also has a tidal indicator. Such watches could only be purchased from Abercrombie & Fitch stores so they have become very rare. This is reflected in its value of $3,000–3,750 (£2,000–2,500).

▶ This 1944 rare stainless steel Patek Philippe wristwatch has a perpetual calendar, moonphase, and indirect centre seconds. It made a record $860,250 (£573,500) when it was sold at Sotheby's in October 1996, against a pre-auction estimate of $150,000–225,000 (£100,000–150,000). The fact that it was the first watch of its type, with indirect centre seconds, to be offered at auction will have been a major factor in it fetching such a high price.

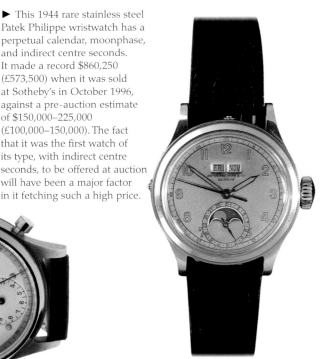

Electronic/Quartz Watches

Early examples of new technology are sought by collectors, and electronic watches are no exception. The model most remembered today is Bulova's Accutron, which, at the time it was made, did not prove to be a great commercial success. Another classic of this type is the digital watch, which simply displays the time using numerals (*see* page 98).

Early electro-mechanical watches like the Hamilton Pacer have a balance wheel that is driven electronically by a battery. Electronic watches have transistorized elements (integrated circuit) but are still battery driven. Such watches, although a vital part of the history of timekeeping, will not necessarily have great value. This is probably due to the styling and the fact that batteries will run out – most collectors want examples that are in working order. Early Omega gold bracelet watches from the 1970s have an auction value of around $1,500 (£1,000), but this is partly due to the fact that they have heavy gold bracelets. An Accutron Spaceview, on the other hand, would fetch only $375–750 (£250–500).

Quartz watches are not in themselves collectable, although some Cartier and Rolex quartz watches are relatively rare. One make that is collectable is the Swatch quartz watch (*see* page 112); there is even a Swatch Collectors Club that caters specifically for this market.

Ladies' Watches

This is a very specialized area that in recent decades, with the growing role the female executive plays in the business world, has expanded due to some manufacturers producing watches with the intricate mechanisms that are more usually found in watches made for men. However, the more collectable ladies' watches are usually a combination of mechanical movements and precious and semi-precious stones, with watches by Cartier, Patek Philippe, Chopard, and Piaget being among the most sought-after.

One enduringly popular form is the gem-set evening or cocktail watch, which first became liked in the 1920s. Some of these have elegant, black-silk cord bracelets, secured by diamond-set lugs, while others are set into an integral bracelet and are regarded as pieces of jewellery. In March 1999, for example, an Art Deco Cartier black onyx-and-diamond bracelet watch, which had a circular portrait-cut diamond rather than a glass above the dial, fetched $60,000 (£40,000) in a jewellery sale at Christie's in London.

The gold watches on expanding bracelets that your mother and grandmother may have worn are not popular today. This is because they are small in size (and therefore are difficult to read at a glance), they have to be wound, and they look old-fashioned.

▲ This *c.*1920 elegant Longines watch sums up why gem-set watches are so collectable. Primarily a piece of jewellery, it is worth $1,125–3,000 (£750–2,000).

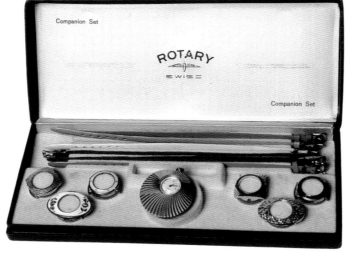

▲ This Rotary Swiss Companion Set is a good surviving example of fashion from the 1950s. The wristwatch comes with interchangeable bezels and straps so that it can be adapted to suit any type of costume or occasion. Such watches have greater appeal to collectors of fashion than watch collectors as they are more novelty items. However, it is nice to see an example in such good condition and this is reflected in its price of $115–130 (£75–85).

Children's and Novelty Watches

This is an area that is ever-growing and it is a great way of introducing children to the world of collecting. The first specific child's watch was the Ingersoll Mickey Mouse watch, which was introduced in 1933 in the USA. Since then there have been many variations depicting favourite cartoon characters, including Dan Dare, Buck Rogers, and Flash Gordon, produced right up to the present day. Watches with advertising logos – such as those produced by Elgin or Hamilton in the 1940s advertising Coca-Cola – can also be collectable. The price range for such pieces is quite wide, starting at under $150 (£100). They really fall more under the label of fashion and design, and are usually collected simply for their novelty value.

A word of warning needs to be given as this is a time in which logos are favoured motifs on all types of goods. Watches that are produced today with such logos are not necessarily going to become the collector's items of the future, unless perhaps they are produced in very small, limited editions. Most of these watches, including those by houses such as Christian Dior, Harley Davidson, and Yves St Laurent are produced as fashion watches; that is they are there to be worn and enjoyed and then discarded when heavy wear starts to show.

One phenomenon of the last two decades has been the Swatch watch. They were designed to be affordable second watches, and from this idea the name swatch was derived. The first Swatches were launched in 1983 and quickly caught the public's imagination. The British fashion designer Vivienne Westwood designed a Pop Swatch, which came in an orb-shaped case and was released in a limited edition of 40,000 (*see* below).

▲ Novelty watches have long been a feature in American watches and are a cheap, accessible collecting area. The Clinton and Peanut watches shown here would appeal not only to watch collectors but also to collectors of advertising and political memorabilia too. They are worth $45–75 (£30–50) each.

► This novelty pocket watch by Heuer has its dial decorated as a roulette wheel and is inscribed with the words Monte Carlo, where there is a world-famous casino. The stopwatch feature would have been used by gamblers as a novel way of choosing roulette numbers. This watch is worth around $225 (£150).

◄ The orb shape of this 1980s plastic watch by Vivienne Westwood is echoed by its box. The few retailers of this watch included Harrods. To collectors it will be as important to have the box in tip-top condition as it will be to have the watch itself. It is worth $400–430 (£265–285).

Some Points to Remember

While the metal of a watch case and its bracelet should be considered, in many cases the desirability and value of the watch lies in its movement, although those with platinum cases are eagerly sought after. Quite often the value of a gold or silver case is limited to its scrap value since collectors look at the overall design and movement as being more important. However, ladies' gem-set watches are different as they are often regarded as items of jewellery in their own right.

In most areas of collecting condition is of prime importance, and this is certainly true with wristwatches. To maintain or increase their current value, particularly if they are of a more recent vintage, wristwatches must be in good working order. Clean, unrestored, and undamaged dials are very important factors to look out for as the more complex dials cannot easily be restored. It is worth remembering that if a serious collector wants to buy a particular watch and is faced with the choice of one with a restored dial or one with a slightly damaged original dial, you will find that in the majority of cases they will go for the one with the damage.

Remember to have any waterproofing checked before you buy as failure to do so can cause serious problems if the watch is worn in water without its proper sealing.

Watches were designed originally to be placed on either a leather strap or some kind of bracelet. While it is impractical to imagine that a watch will still have its original leather strap – since leather is a perishable commodity – the buckle on older watches may well have some identifying marks to show that it is the original, or it may be made from the same precious metal as the watch case. It is important in such an event to make sure that the original buckle is reused each time a new strap is required. Metal bracelets should always be of the same metal or mixture of metals as the watch case. Very often original bracelets will be marked with the name or logo of the watch maker.

Finding Out More About the Subject

It is important to read up on the subject as widely as possible before going out into the marketplace. There is a wide variety of books on the subject (*see* the bibliography on page 155) so you can easily get a basic understanding and feel for what you are going to pursue. Auction catalogues and the catalogues and

◀ Steel Chronograph, *c.*1945
This watch ideally illustrates how important condition is since it has a very complicated telemeter dial. This is a good, early example, but if it had had any damage it would have been very difficult to restore as the watch has flyback centre seconds and continuous seconds as well as minute recording subsidiary dials. Always check condition carefully before buying as it affects the price considerably. (Examples may fetch $525–1,875/£350–1,250.)

▶ Cyma watch from *c.*1940
At first glance you could dismiss this watch as not being very valuable (because the makers are of no particular note and there are no special features), but on a closer inspection you will see that it is in unused condition. It actually comes from unsold stock and so both the case and movement are in mint condition. This is something that is very appealing to a collector and means that the watch should hold its value extremely well – possibly fetching around $750 (£500) if sold today.

pamphlets produced by leading watch manufacturers are also good sources of information. Magazines such as *International Wristwatch* and *QP* are also worth reading. Once you have started collecting keep on reading because new information comes to light and new trends are constantly revealed, which helps you keep abreast of the current market. No expert will ever tell you that they know all that there is to know about a subject, and new articles and books help all to keep on top of their subject.

Museums are also good places to visit in order to learn more (*see* p153). Many of the watch manufacturers have their own in-house museum, which often can be viewed by prior arrangement. The growth of watches as a fashion item means that you will also find examples in design, and other, museums.

The Marketplace

You should remember that, like stocks and shares and many other investments, the value of a watch or collection of watches is subject to gains and losses. This can be due to many factors, such as a change in what is perceived as fashionable, a glut on the market, and, of course, changes to the economic situation in a country, or globally. It is because of this that you should never buy for short-term investment. While it is advisable to buy for the pleasures of personal ownership of beautiful, practical, and wearable pieces it is obvious that a sudden increase in value can make the sale of a watch seem like an attractive prospect. However, before you sell you should really think through the impact the sale may have on your collection and realize that you may never be able to replace that particular watch at a later date, whether due to cost or rarity. It can be easy to sell on the spur of the moment and repent thereafter. Some collectors do decide that they wish to change from one area of specialization to another, and when such dispersals occur it provides a great opportunity for other collectors to acquire pieces to start or enrich their collection.

It is a changeable market and a collector must really know and understand the market, particularly when thinking in terms of investment. The more unusual the watch the more likelihood it has of retaining its appeal to other collectors. In the 1980s large yellow-gold watches such as the gemset Rolex President were regarded as the pinnacle of status. Today there is a definite move away from such ostentation. Simpler, cleaner lines are preferred, as is white gold or platinum. Good names with complicated mechanisms and dials are popular now, and there is still a very active market for the more masculine, thick watches such as those made by Breitling, IWC, and TAG Heuer.

So where should you go to buy? There are several options as the wristwatch market is a widespread one, with collectors found in Europe (especially Germany, Italy, and the United Kingdom), the USA, and the Far East. While the Western markets, including the USA, are very particular about condition, the same is not true at the present time in the Far Eastern market, where restoration is acceptable. This is because the collectors' interest there is chiefly concerned with new or relatively contemporary models, particularly if gem-set.

Auctions

Many of the major auction houses hold specialist sales of clocks and watches in which wristwatches are included. If they are selling a large collection then there may well be a specialist wristwatch sale. And do not forget that gem-set watches may be included in jewellery sales. Prices achieved at auction for watches that are still available in the retail market are somewhere between 25 per cent and a third of the current shop price. For example, an 18-carat gold Breitling Montbrillant QP (automatic with perpetual calendar and chronograph), made in a limited edition of one hundred and retailing at $36,375 (£24,250) in the shops, was sold at Bonhams recently for $9,750 (£6,500).

If you are looking for a particular model it may well be worth waiting for one to come up at auction, but remember you may have to wait years if it is a rare piece. Do remember that if you are buying in the auction saleroom you will have competition from other buyers. Sometimes keen rivalry will achieve very high prices, which may not always be relevant to the true value of the watch. So make sure you always set yourself a limit and do not allow yourself to get carried away.

Dealers

While admittedly you will more than likely pay more if you go to a specialist dealer, when you first start collecting this is perhaps the safest place to buy from as certain safeguards are already in place. For example, the watch will be in working order, you will get a full descriptive invoice of your purchase, and should there be any problems you will be able to go back to the dealer to sort them out. It is a good idea to build up a relationship with a dealer, who will be able to guide you in the formative stages of your collecting. If you are specializing in a particular type or make of watch then a dealer's help and advice can prove very useful. They will also try and find watches for you and, as your collection grows, you may well be able to trade things back to them should you wish to.

Internet

You will find wristwatches for sale over the internet on sites like eBay and individual dealers' sites. Such dealers will provide a full description, and preferably an image, of the watches that they are selling. Most good sites will respond quickly to emails so don't be afraid to ask lots of questions about the watches on offer. Sometimes it is possible to barter the price down a bit, especially if you

◄ It is important to learn how to read auction houses' catalogues, as what is left out of a description can often be as important as what is put in. You should always be sure to research the terms and conditions used by such houses. These catalogues, as well as specialist magazines such as *International Wristwatch*, are a good way of keeping up with market trends and prices. They build up into a practical and informative reference library for the serious collector.

keep emails brief and friendly. The watches displayed should have plenty of close-up pictures available, and in some cases this can show the condition in greater detail than when using a watchmaker's glass. As with any dealer, establish a guarantee period for the watch and try and get a returns policy established in case the watch arrives not as described or shown in the photos. Most watches in internet sales are newer ones and in good condition, so the experienced buyers know what they are getting. However, for more important pieces it may be better to examine them in person instead.

Other Sources

You will find second-hand and collectable wristwatches on sale in many antique markets, watch fairs, and even boot sales, but these are not places for someone with an untrained eye to go out and purchase a watch from. You will possibly find a bargain or a rare watch because not all those selling the watches will have the necessary knowledge, but of course you will only recognize that treasure if you have built up your own knowledge. Remember that you are buying the watch "as seen", so you have no guarantee that it is in working order.

Caring for Wristwatches

How should you take care of a watch once you have bought it? The following are points to consider.

It is important, since watches are so portable and therefore easily stolen, to keep a photographic record of watches in your collection.

For overhauls and restoration always go to a specialist watch workshop and keep receipts for cleaning or restoration work. These, together with any receipts, packaging, and booklets from the original purchase,

◀ This shows a Rolex box, certificate, and seal – these are all part of the original packaging and provide proof of provenance. Although they will make a watch more expensive to purchase, look after such items as they will also help retain its value.

provide part of the watch's history. They show proof that good care has been taken and may well help the watch increase or maintain its value. In the event of buying a watch without its bracelet or strap they will help to identify what type of strap it had originally.

If you do not have the original or another suitable box or case, watches can be stored on fabric rolls or in acid-free tissue paper. Some collectors keep them in special cabinets with fitted drawers. Cases mainly can be kept clean by the occasional gentle polish with a soft cloth. You should never use anything abrasive.

A mechanical or automatic watch should be wound at least once a month. If an automatic wristwatch has not been worn for a while wind it between 35 and 40 times to build up the full power, which then will be maintained by normal wear. You can buy battery-driven winding boxes for both automatic and hand-wound watches. Although expensive they are practical, as some movements can take 20 minutes to set. Batteries in quartz watches must be changed as soon as the watch stops. The supply of batteries for certain movements could some day run out so always make sure you have spares.

▼ A watch glass is a useful tool for collectors to use to look at the movement and dial in close detail. The black glass shown here is the most common type – the Cartier limited-edition glass is collectable in its own right.

▲ An over-the-shoulder view of a watchmaker working on a movement. It is always best to get professionals to look at watches that need to be repaired or cleaned, as they have the right tools and specialist skills.

◄ It is important to keep watches in working order and some collectors prefer to use an automatic winding box, such as this Orbita wind-up box, to keep their watch going.

Prices

The prices used in this book are based on what you may expect to pay if you were to purchase the watches new through a retailer or, if older, what would be a fair price if buying from a dealer. Where prices reflect those found in an auction or internet sale this is indicated. In all cases, other than when purchased new, the prices can only be an indication of what you might have to pay, since condition and other factors outlined in this book will affect the price of any individual watch.

Fakes and Replicas

There is a distinct difference between fakes and replicas in the world of wristwatches. A replica is something that is a modern reproduction of a wristwatch and, while it may look exactly like the original piece, it will not have all the working parts and the materials used will not, usually, be of the same quality or substance as the original. Replicas are usually sold as such and their prices reflect that fact. There are indeed sites where such watches are sold at prices that clearly indicate that they are not originals. A fake, on the other hand, is a replica that is sold with the clear intent to deceive. It will be sold at a knock-down price. If, for

example, you are told that a watch costs $450 (£300) but you can have it for $150 (£100), alarm bells should ring.

Among the replicas and fakes around are examples of Patek Philippe, Cartier, Chopard, TAG Heuer, and Omega. Even cheaper brands including Swatch can be copied, and vintage models such as Rolex Bubble Backs, Princes, and Jaeger Reversos have been faked. Don't be deceived if the watch is made of precious metal, as gold cases have been cast from originals and sold as real. Always buy from a reputable dealer who will give a written guarantee, or an auction house that will authenticate.

Rolex

Rolex is probably one of the most well-known makers of wristwatches and it certainly has a strong market appeal to all ages. It is the allure of cashing in on such popularity that has attracted fakers around the world to try and get a slice of the action. Certainly the makers of these fakes have got more serious about the business and over the years have got cleverer in their copies. Nowadays they have replicated the effect of the genuine Rolex sweeping hand but are not yet able

to copy the Rolex method of stopping the second hand when the winding crown is pulled out for time-setting. Genuine Rolexes now have a quick date-setting function so it is no longer necessary to turn the hands for a full 24 hours. Remember that a fake Rolex can be presented with appropriate cases and other paraphernalia (which may be the real thing, or yet more faking) – so do your homework to ensure that you know enough to recognize the real thing.

Faces

▲ **Genuine GMT Rolex**
The first thing that strikes you about this watch is its quality and the harmonious scale of everything on the dial. A genuine Rolex GMT Master has a bezel that turns, which is a feature found on many of their sports models. The bezels are securely fitted, and when you turn them there should be a total of 60 clicks.

▲ **Fake Rolex GMT Master**
The bezels on a fake are usually much looser and in some fakes the notches are much larger than those on an original. The hour markers, the hands, and the lettering are all slightly heavier than those on an original. The fake, although good quality, lacks the finesse of the original. The reverse of this fake is shown on page 21.

▲ **Fake Rolex Explorer II**
Rolex watches with a date aperture are fitted with a special magnifying bubble over the date. The Rolex magnification is 2.5, while those on fakes is just over half that. If you look at the date on this fake Explorer II and the date on the genuine GMT Master to the left you will see the difference clearly. The reverse of this fake is shown on the top of page 21.

▲ **Fake Rolex Cellini**
At first glance this could be taken for the real thing. The markings on the dial are correct but a closer look at the case reveals a slightly brassy, cold look. This is indicative of the case being 24-carat gold-plated – real Cellini watches are made in 18-carat gold. Always check for signs of wear around the case edge – if it is a fake you may see signs of the steel case showing underneath.

Backs

▲ The same model number is used on the first two fakes here.

▲ The familiar green hologram label is found on good fakes.

▲ An original Cellini would be all gold, and have no engraving.

◄ Genuine Rolexes have a green hologram label with the Rolex crown and model number. The case back below them will usually not be engraved, although you may come across some ladies' models with "ORIGINAL ROLEX DESIGN" engraved on the back. It is also important to know what materials particular models are made from; for example, Rolex have never made any watches with a crystal back.

Bracelets

▲ Note the difference in quality and crispness between these two fakes. Rolex actually supply replacement bracelets, which have a considerable retail value, so always be wary if someone offers you a Rolex with a replica bracelet.

▲ Do not underestimate the skills of the faker. Nowadays they take care to ensure that markings, even on the inside of the clasp, look authentic. The quality and weight of the bracelet is also important – a genuine steel Rolex is slightly heavier than these fakes.

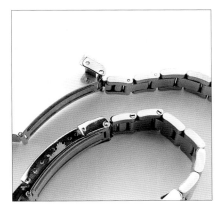

▲ Remember that any extension links to a Rolex bracelet are attached with small screws. Normally fakes will have flat pins, although in the case of better-quality fakes they use pins with split ends, as here, so that they resemble screwheads.

Movements

▲ The genuine movement is the Rolex calibre 3175; this fake has a simple automatic movement.

Winders and Bezels

Well-made bezel that moves with precision; the fake bezels are much looser.

The moulding on these fake crowns is not as crisp as the genuine examples.

Plain, unsigned winding rotor.

▲ On a genuine Rolex the winding crown will screw down in a precise manner – most fakes will not. The seal should also be visible when the winding crown is unscrewed.

International Watch Company (IWC)

IWC's GST range of watches was launched in 1997 and was designed specifically for sportsmen. As GSTs are quite modern there aren't as many fakes around as there are for other watches. GSTs are highly masculine in character, with clear, simple lines. They also come in a range of models. These include pressure-treated diving watches such as the GST Deep One, which is featured in the photographs below. The GST Perpetual Calendar model has a perpetual moonphase as well as the calendar, and the GST Chrono-Rattrapante has split seconds hands that allow intermediate timing. The GST Aquatimer was added to the range in 1998, as was the GST Automatic Alarm, which has a mechanical alarm system. The name GST is made up of the initials of the three metals that are used in the production of these watches – gold, steel, and titanium. These metals reflect the ruggedness of the watches, and the demands that they face. Titanium's qualities as a metal, which include its light weight and strength, make it ideally suitable for many purposes and IWC were quick to spot and exploit its uses in the world of watchmaking.

The GST Deep One was first produced in 1999 and it has some remarkable features that are invaluable to serious divers. It can, for example, show the time that the wearer spends beneath water, and can also indicate the depth to which the wearer dived.

Faces

▲ The genuine IWC watch has a black dial that contrasts well against the yellow hour hand. The small seconds hand has a stop function. The revolving inner ring shows the length of time the dive has taken and the watch can measure the dive depth down to 45 metres.

▲ On the fake GST Deep One the dial is white and the hour hand is red. There is no hand to show immersion depth. The button for the setting ring and the immersion valve are purely decorative in this case.

Backs

▲ The back of a genuine GST Deep One is engraved with "International Watch Co Schaffhausen" in raised letters. The centre of the back has a special patented lock that has a distinctive central design.

▲ The back of the fake, while engraved with the correct wording, is surface-engraved rather than raised, and also has IWC engraved at the centre of the back cover. The screw cover, too, is wrong – it is of a standard type, rather than the special IWC patented one.

Bracelets

► The IWC GST Deep One is designed to be worn by divers to a depth of 100 metres and can be used both in lake and sea diving. The button at 4 o'clock, with a slightly raised crown, can be adjusted to reflect the appropriate atmospheric pressure for the depth gauge. It is easy to shorten or lengthen the genuine bracelet as, unlike standard metal bracelets, its design does not include screws. The fakes are not designed in the same way.

▲ A genuine IWC bracelet has a special, patented, push-button release system.

▲ This fake bracelet can only be shortened by a limited amount, where the screws can be seen.

• *The fish is the IWC symbol to indicate that a watch is water-resistant. It can be seen on both the genuine and fake.*

• *The inlet valve, the one with the slightly higher crown, is purely decorative on the fake watch, as is the setting ring. Only the central winding crown is functional.*

• *The genuine watch comes with a small pump so that the diver can test the watch before using it.*

How Watches Work

Anyone who seriously collects something with moving parts, such as a car, clock, or scientific instrument, is going to be interested in understanding how it works. This is certainly true of the wristwatch collector. Knowledge of wristwatch movements, whether simple or complicated, is an integral part of understanding what you are buying, and over a period of time you should be able to judge whether a movement is in good order or not. This section provides an overview of some of the movements and features you will come across and explains exactly how they work.

Mechanical Movements

A mechanical watch is a device for keeping time that uses energy from a wound spring that is released through a set of gears and an escapement. It differs from a quartz watch because it uses mechanical components. Most mechanical watches are fitted with a Swiss lever movement. The diagram to the right is a variation of the first lever movement, which was invented *c*.1759 by the English watchmaker Thomas Mudge. Nowadays, while certain of the more important firms will make their own movements, there are specialist firms that make both mechanical and quartz movements, quartz being the most commonly produced.

The mechanical movement is the thing that attracts the collector, and so it is important to know a little more about how it works. A Swiss lever movement will have over 80 different parts to it. To the wearer or collector of such a watch their daily contact with the movement comes through turning the crown – the winding button. The crown is attached to the winding stem, which in turn is attached to the wheels and pinions of the winding train. These wheels and pinions give the mainspring, which is contained within a barrel, its going power. To prevent the mainspring unwinding through the winding mechanism there is a small pawl, known as a click, on the ratchet wheel – you will hear it clicking as the watch is wound.

Once the mainspring is wound it is ready to drive the movement and the hands. This is done through the going train, again a series of pinions and wheels, which has a reduction gear that is set so that the train's fourth wheel – the seconds wheel – revolves completely every 60 seconds. The mainspring needs to be stopped from unwinding too quickly and this is done by the escape wheel, which is situated at the end of the going train. The escape wheel is connected

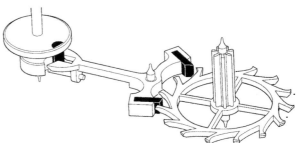

▲ **Swiss lever movement**
The escapement, with jewelled pallet working in and out of the escape wheel; as the balance swings the impulse jewel acts on the pallet fork.

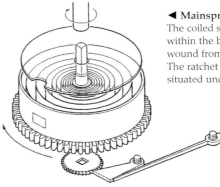

◄ **Mainspring barrel**
The coiled spring is contained within the brass barrel and is wound from the centre arbor. The ratchet and click are situated underneath the spring.

to the pallet and it is via this that small pulses of energy are sent to the balance wheel (an oscillator that controls the movement's speed). The escape wheel and balance wheel, therefore, control the release of energy from the mainspring and this regulated release forms the basis of the watch's accuracy as a timekeeper.

Where there are heavy points of friction between the metal components of the movement you will find bearings, known as jewels – hence the term jewelled lever. Although originally real rubies and sapphires were used, today the jewels are usually made of man-made corundum. However, in less expensive movements steel pins are used, and these movements are known as pin-lever movements.

Automatic Movements

The search to find an automatic system for winding a watch started in the 18th century, and the first self-winding pocket watch was made by Swiss horologist Abraham-Louis Perrelet *c*.1770. Improvements and refinements to Perrelet's concept were made by Breguet in the early 1780s. The first successful self-winding wristwatch was introduced in 1922 by Leon Leroy. The oscillating weight needed to self-wind the watch is normally in the shape of a rotor that has a 360° swing (although Leroy's original was a pointed oval shape). This swings with the movement of the wrist and comes to a stop at the lowest point. It needs to be kept fully wound, which may involve manual winding, to maintain full power and good timekeeping.

Electric/Quartz Watches

The development of the electric watch began in the 1950s. The first electronic watches used a conventional balance wheel powered by a battery. These were made obsolete in the '60s by the tuning fork, introduced in the Accutron watch. However, the continuing pursuit of the miniaturization of batteries in both Japan and Switzerland then led to the production of the first quartz movement, in 1968. While today we are used to the classically styled design of wristwatch with a quartz movement, designers in the late 1960s thought that the time should be shown in a more "interesting way". What resulted was bulky watches with either liquid crystal display or light-emitting diodes (LCD or LED), which were produced for a while before public demand moved back in favour of more conventional forms. The power source that drives such watches is of course the battery, usually silver-oxide or lithium. The electric current vibrates the quartz crystal at a rate of 32,768 vibrations (known as Hertz) per second.

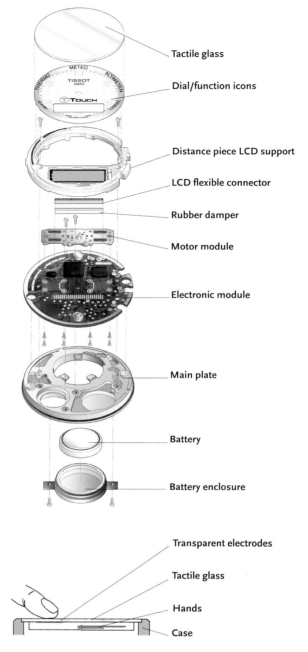

Tactile glass

Dial/function icons

Distance piece LCD support

LCD flexible connector

Rubber damper

Motor module

Electronic module

Main plate

Battery

Battery enclosure

Transparent electrodes

Tactile glass

Hands

Case

▲ The latest Swiss technological developments can be seen in the Tissot T Touch. Illustrated above are all the component parts so you can see how the transparent electrodes are activated when the glass over the dial is touched. Instead of having to remember which button to press you simply have to touch the screen for the feature you require (which include a compass and altimeter).

▲ Cufflink Watches
There have been huge developments within the watchmaking world. One has been the making of a quartz movement small enough to fit inside these *c*.1996 cufflinks. These will no doubt appeal to collectors of the future because of their originality.

► Chronograph button
One of the most important features of the chronograph is the button that controls the actions of the timing devices, including bringing the hands back to zero. Some waterproof chronographs even have screw-down buttons, the same as the winding crown.

◄ Chronograph close-up
This close-up allows us to see the different functions found on a Breitling Navitimer, which has a bi-directional bezel, a calculator, sweep-second, hour, and minutes hands, and the subsidiary dials for seconds, minutes, and hours.

action of the movement. One special type of calendar watch is the perpetual calendar. Perpetual calendar watches have been adjusted to cope with the changes of the Gregorian calendar (introduced in 1582), but on 28th February 2100, which is not a leap year, adjustments will have to be made either manually or by the replacement of a small piece of the mechanism.

Moonphases are indicated by a disc with 59 teeth (lunar periods are 29.5 days). The disc has two moons on it, opposite one another, so as the movement turns the disc the moons will show the lunar phases in succession through a lunar-shaped panel in the dial. The complete cycle for the two moons takes 59 days.

▼ Patek Moonphase, 1944
Here we can see clearly the discs used for day and month, as well as the moonphase disc with its two moons and 59 teeth around the edge.

Additional Features

Just as the movements of pocket watches were developed and improved upon by watchmakers over the centuries, so too was the wristwatch. Special features such as those listed below were originally often found in pocket watches but were utilized in wristwatches too – they bear testimony to the skill of those making them, especially when you remember that wristwatches are smaller in size than pocket watches.

Anti-Magnetism

Magnetic fields abound in the course of our daily life from domestic electrical equipment and so on. To prevent such magnetic forces having a detrimental effect on a watch's mechanism, many of the metal parts of a movement are made from metal alloys.

Calendars and Moonphases

The ability to tell the day, date, and month is another feature found on many wristwatches. These can be shown either by a combination of apertures for the day and month in the centre of the dial, or the date being shown by a hand pointing to the dates on the edge of the dial, or by three apertures. One particular feature that is also nice to find with a calendar watch is a moonphase, which gives details of the lunar month. This feature can be included in the watch's movement as it is possible to make the necessary astronomical calculations.

The day or date display in calendar watches is activated by a wheel or discs that are engaged by the

Chronographs

These are watches with a central seconds hand that acts as a stopwatch. Although the search for such watches started in the 1820s, the basic principles used today date from 1862. The chronograph movement has a heart-shaped cam that enables the seconds hand and, where applicable, minute or hour registers, to return to zero immediately when the button or slide on the side of the watch case is pressed. This seconds hand is used to time short-term events. Some more complex chronographs have two central seconds hands, which means that two different things can be timed at once.

Dials

In order that troops could see their watches at night, watches with luminous hands and figures were introduced during World War I. This early luminescence was created by a mixture that included radioactive salt among its ingredients. This was eventually banned from use in the 1950s and tritium, which has lower radioactivity, was used instead.

Another way of "illuminating" a dial in the dark involves coating the hands and numerals with a special material that, when exposed to a light source for a time, will remain luminous for up to eight hours. Another system is used in the Indiglo watches produced by Timex; when a button is pressed on the side of the case minute currents are transmitted from a battery and react with electrodes set in the dial to produce light.

Power Reserve

A device invented by Breguet that shows how much power is left in a watch's mainspring – the more power the better the timekeeping will be. Like the indicator on a car's petrol tank, as the watch unwinds the power reserve indicator goes down, showing how little power is left.

Shock Protection

An Incabloc system is a widely used, patented anti-shock system that protects a watch's rate from varying if it is dropped on a hard surface. Usually the endstones and jewel-bearings of the pivots are spring mounted so that they can absorb any shocks. The accepted test is dropping the watch from a height of 3 feet (1 metre) onto some form of hard surface.

Striking Mechanisms

Some movements have features that were originally found in old pocket watches. One highly sought-after example is the minute repeater, which is regarded by most collectors as the ultimate wristwatch, even though they probably will not be able to afford the astronomical prices such watches command. Such mechanisms are the product of the watchmaker's art. They are complicated mechanisms that trigger off hammers – with a minute repeater, the watch is fitted with a striking mechanism that, at the press of a button, will strike the hours, quarters, and minutes on at least two sets of different gongs. The quarter repeater strikes the hours and quarters to the last quarter. An alarm mechanism is similar and works when the hands reach the appropriate time.

Waterproofing

Some watches are designed to be worn in or under water. Their glasses and the back of the cases are tight-fitting and some will have a waterproof seal, which also helps to keep dust out in normal terrestrial wear. Watches designed for deep-sea diving will have special additional features to cope with the underwater pressure, in some cases having helium release valves.

When Rolex invented the Oyster the company patented the screw-down crown mechanism. The winding crown was always the most vulnerable part on a watch as water could get in through the stem. Now we have watches which can go even to the greatest depths, up to 33,000 feet (11,100 metres).

World Time

The growth in air and sea travel, especially by businessmen, led to the development in the 1930s of watches that could indicate the time in various cities and time zones around the world. The world is divided into 24 time zones and world timer watches are fitted with special mechanisms so that they can show the time in each of these.

History of Wristwatches

Pre-1910

Knowing the time has always been important, and the story of the watch from the 16th century onwards is full of new developments and scientific know-how. The wristwatch has really only featured in that story for the last hundred years. Before then those who could afford them used pocket watches. These went from the large bulky double-cased verge-escapement watches of the 17th and 18th centuries to the slimmer, cylinder, and lever-escapement watches of the 19th century and onwards.

The demand for wristwatches seems to have originated with 19th-century well-to-do ladies who wanted watches that could be seen easily. They wanted timekeepers that were not hidden among the fabric of their clothing, and so the first types of watch to be worn around the wrist emerged. These were, in fact, adaptations of fob (pendant) watches, which were watches suspended from a small brooch-type bar. Some were encased in a protective leather case, mounted on a leather strap, and could be worn when out riding or hunting. It is the watches that were mounted into bracelets of precious metals that are the most eagerly sought by collectors today. These were often enamelled or decorated with precious and semi-precious stones and were rightly regarded as pieces of jewellery. One fine early example, which can be seen at Hillwood Museum in Washington DC, has an elaborate gold bracelet set with enamel miniatures of Czar Nicholas I and his wife, a suitably appropriate touch since it was an Imperial gift.

Men were quite happy to continue to use pocket watches and it was well into the 1930s before the wristwatch became the more usual form of watch worn by a man. This does not mean that there were no wristwatches for male use before then. Indeed, officers of the German Navy were supplied with wristwatches by the Swiss firm Girard-Perregaux in the last two decades of the 19th century. And in 1904 the Brazilian pioneer aviator Alberto Santos-Dumont persuaded his friend the jeweller Louis Cartier to design a wristwatch for him. It became known as the Santos and was put into commercial production some seven years later.

It can be argued convincingly that the true story of the wristwatch, as we know it, is a story of the 20th century. Its design and function, while being influenced by historical, social, and sporting events over the succeeding decades, has ultimately remained the same – an instrument to tell the time accurately.

▶ A silver-and-blue enamel pendant watch, c.1900, by the Swiss firm C. Bucherer; the enamel decoration reflects the Art Nouveau period. It would have been worn suspended from a chain around the neck. Any damage to the enamel will diminish the value of such pieces.
$600–900 (£400–600)

▶ The first wristwatches were fob watches encased in leather wrist straps, making them easier to use. This particular example is from the International Clock Museum in Switzerland.
$300–500 (£450–750)

◀ This Swiss-lever movement, signed "Rotherhams", is rare as it can be worn in different ways and shows the transition from pendant to wristwatch.
$2,250–3,000 (£1,500–2,000)

E. DENT AND CO.,

MANUFACTURERS OF

WATCHES, CHRONOMETERS,

ASTRONOMICAL, TURRET, AND OTHER CLOCKS

(CATALOGUES ON APPLICATION).

TO
HER MAJESTY,

TO H.R.H.
THE PRINCE OF WALES,

AND FOREIGN SOVEREIGNS.

MAKERS OF THE GREAT WESTMINSTER CLOCK (BIG BEN); OF THE STANDARD CLOCK
OF THE ROYAL OBSERVATORY, GREENWICH; AND OF STANDARD
CLOCKS IN MOST PRINCIPAL BRITISH, FOREIGN,
AND COLONIAL OBSERVATORIES.

ONLY PLACES OF BUSINESS:
61, STRAND, AND 34, ROYAL EXCHANGE, LONDON.

GRAVÉ D'APRÈS PHOTOGRAPHIE

OMEGA

Vue de l'usine de la maison Louis Brandt et frère à Bienne.

► The Omega 12, launched in 1900, was the first wristwatch made by Omega. Its small size and centre lugs are typical of the period. Such watches were designed initially for women. $450–750 (£300–500)

► 18-carat gold cushion-shaped wristwatch, signed Tiffany & Co, c.1908. Like many jewellers on both sides of the Atlantic, Tiffany bought its watch movements from Swiss watchmakers, in this case Patek Philippe. $7,500–9,000 (£5,000–6,000)

◄ An oversized single-button left-handed Swiss chronograph, 1910. Very few manufacturers catered for left-handed people, which means this particular watch is very rare – as reflected in its relatively high value. $2,250–3,000 (£1,500–2,000)

▼ Louis Brandt 13, 1892. This museum piece is the first minute-repeating wristwatch, which was made by the Swiss firm of Louis Brandt et Fils. $15,000–30,000 (£10,000–20,000)

❍ 1675 A balance spring suitable for watches was invented by Dr Robert Hook.
❍ 1770 The first self-winding pocket watch was developed by Abraham-Louis Perrelet.
❍ 1795 The Swiss-born watchmaker Abraham-Louis Breguet (1747–1823), who worked in Paris, invented the tourbillon.

❍ 1867 An inexpensive pin-pallet escapement movement was invented by Georg-Friedrich Roskopf – it then went into mass-production in 1870.
❍ 1885 The Waltham watch-making company was founded in Waltham, Massachusetts.
❍ 1892 The first minute-repeating wristwatch was made for Louis Brandt & Co.

❍ 1892 The American company Hamilton was founded.
❍ 1902 Synthetic rubies were made for the first time and were soon used for movement bearings.
❍ 1906 The Swiss watch manufacturer Certina advertised its first ladies' wristwatches.
❍ 1908 The Rolex trademark was registered in London by Hans Wilsdorf.

1910s

The early 20th century is often looked back upon as a halcyon period since it was a time of relative peace. This dream was to be shattered in 1914 by the outbreak of World War I, which changed the way many people lived forever.

Men's wristwatches really began to be developed during World War I. In the mud of the trenches and no-man's land it was certainly more practical and potentially safer to wear a watch on the wrist where it could be seen easily rather than having to struggle to extricate a pocket watch from a uniform pocket.

Many of these early wristwatches were in fact converted half-hunter pocket watches (watches whose outer cover has enamelled figures around a central glass aperture through which the hands and part of the dial can be seen, enabling the wearer to tell the time). These were converted using the addition of lugs through which a strap could be attached. However, the dials on such conversions did not face the wearer when on the wrist, and subsequently they are less valuable and desirable today than purpose-made examples that have their dials in the normal position.

Strap watches converted from pocket watches will also often have engine-turned or chased decoration on the reverse; features not found on a true wristwatch.

It was during this period that Swiss and American manufacturers started producing Trench wristwatches, on which the dial and glass were covered by a protective metal grille. Watches with luminous hands and numerals were also developed, which made it easier for troops to see the time in the dark. Switzerland's neutrality allowed it to continue the development of the wristwatch, and indeed both world wars saw Swiss manufacturers producing huge numbers of watches for armed forces on either side of the conflicts. Many of these are eagerly sought-after today, especially if they were never used. Incidentally, the famous Cartier "Tank" watch of 1917 was influenced by the first British tanks from 1916 (*see* page 57).

The design for ladies' watches in this period included lozenge, oval, and elliptical shapes. Among the more unusual watches was the "Polyplan", by Movado. This came in elongated oval or rectangular shapes designed to fit the contour of the wrist.

◀ Swiss nickel export watch, *c*.1913. Longines produced this watch specifically for a Turkish retailer and both companies' names appear on the dial. Its Arabic numerals are luminous, which was already a common feature from about 1890 onwards. $450–750 (£300–500).

◀ Movado watch *c*.1915. In 1912 Movado introduced the Polyplan, a wristwatch that fitted the curve of the wrist. It had a specially designed movement on three planes to follow the curve. It is unusual in having the winder at the 12 o'clock position at the top of the watch. $3,200–3,800 (£2,150–2,550).

◄ At first glance this would appear to be a half-hunter pocket watch that has been converted to a wristwatch. However, the positioning of the dial and winding crown, as well as the luminous numerals and hands, show that this was specially made in 1917 with its protective cover, probably for military use. $300–450 (£200–300).

▼ Wire-lug wristwatch with shrapnel cover, c.1916. This Omega "Trench" watch has a grille-like cover that was intended to protect the watch from shrapnel. The enamel dial also bears the inscription "Signal Corps USA". $600–900 (£400–600)

▲ 18-carat gold Officer's watch by Patek Philippe, c.1910. This type of Patek Philippe wristwatch, with hinged case and luminous hands and numerals, is known as the Officer's watch as it was made frequently for military personnel. Both the movement and dial are signed Patek Philippe and the dial also bears the name of the retailer, Tiffany & Co. $7,500–10,500 (£5,000–7,000)

▲ 18-carat gold Cartier Tank watch, 1919. This watch has an engine-turned silver dial. Inspired by British tanks from World War I, such watches have remained enduringly popular – versions are still produced today. Vintage examples such as this will fetch $4,500–7,500 (£3,000–5,000).

○ **1910 The Swiss firm of Longines started making wristwatches for the first time.**
○ **1910 Rolex was awarded the first timekeeping certificate for a mass-produced watch by the Bienne Test Centre in Switzerland.**
○ **1911 The Cartier Santos watch was produced for general sale (*see* page 28).**

○ **1911 Ebel watch brand was started in La-Chaux-de-Fonds by Eugéne and Alice Blum.**
○ **1912 Movado introduced its first wristwatch for military use. The dial and glass were covered with a protective grille.**
○ **1914 The first alarm wristwatch was made by Eterna to a design they had patented in 1908.**
○ **1914 Rolex was awarded a**

Class A timing certificate for its wristwatches by Kew Observatory, London, England.
○ **1917 Omega supplied wristwatches to Great Britain's Royal Flying Corps.**
○ **1918 Omega supplied wristwatches to the United States Army.**
○ **1918 The first synthetic shatterproof watch crystals were made.**

1920s

It is not hard to imagine the impact that World War I had on the world. The huge loss of life among those fighting had a social and economic impact on all strata of society – those who survived wished for a brighter life and tried to forget those four grim years.

The inter-war years are known as the Jazz Age. During this time life seemed to be enjoyed at a frenetic pace. In architecture and the decorative arts the style known as Art Deco dominated the period. It was a style that was not just the preserve of the rich as its influence can be seen in utilitarian objects too. In a 1924 edition of *The Watchmaker* (*Der Uhrmacher*) magazine Leopold Reverchon wrote, "Today it can be said that the wristwatch has conquered the world; it is worn by the woman worker every bit as much as by the society lady; it is particularly popular among the middle classes".

Watch cases definitely reflected the geometric style characteristic of Art Deco and there was a surge of rectangular cases in particular. In fact, the rectangular shape found on both ladies' and men's watches remained popular until the 1950s, when the circular shape once more became prevalent. The shape of chronographs, which were popular for driving, flying, and sporting events, was principally round but, as with many things, there are always exceptions and so

you may come across square examples (*see* page 69). The Swiss firm Mido's productions reflected the search for unusual shapes that mirrored the interests of the period – among its pendant and pocket watches at this time were those in the shape of footballs or planes.

The search for technical excellence continued and in 1929 Jaeger-LeCoultre produced the 2 Ligne, which is the smallest wristwatch with a mechanical movement. Its small size meant that it could be incorporated easily into bracelet designs, and indeed one of its most famous wearers is HRH Queen Elizabeth II.

This decade also saw the production of the first automatic wristwatch. It was the brainchild of English watchmaker John Harwood. He patented the design in 1924 in England and then two years later again in Switzerland. In that country he found a watch manufacturer, Fortis, which was prepared to make his watch. Since it did not have the usual winding crown and stem, the hands were set by turning the bezel – to empower the movement the watch had to be shaken. It was not well received by the watch-buying public, although manufacture of it did go on until 1931. However, it is significant because it sewed the seed for other manufacturers to produce their own self-winding watches in the future.

►► Harwood self-winding watch. This is the earliest example of a self-winding (automatic) watch. This design was patented by the English watchmaker John Harwood in 1924. $750–1,125 (£500–750)

► Hamilton Coronado *c.*1928. The stylized Arabic numerals and black enamel bezel of this gold wristwatch is typical of Hamilton designs in the 1920s. The condition of the enamel is important to collectors as damage will affect the value. $3,000–3,375 (£2,000–2,250)

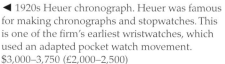

◄ 1920s Heuer chronograph. Heuer was famous for making chronographs and stopwatches. This is one of the firm's earliest wristwatches, which used an adapted pocket watch movement. $3,000–3,750 (£2,000–2,500)

◄ Longines 18-carat gold seconds chronograph, late 1920s/early 1930s. With its distinctive hinged lugs this watch was designed for comfort of wear as the strap wraps closely around the wrist. Longines was famous for its high-quality chronographs. $2,250–3,300 (£1,500–2,200)

► Distinctive cushion-case Rolex Oyster, 1929. This has a prominent screw-down crown. $2,250–3,000 (£1,500–2,000)

► Hamilton Piping Rock. An eagerly sought-after watch, both in the 1920s and today. The simplicity of the design, with its enamelled bezel and Roman numerals, adds to its appeal. $1,500–2,250 (£1,000–1,500)

► Rolex 9-carat wristwatch. The cushion-shape of this watch is typical of the 1920s and was regarded as the height of fashion. This type of watch is very collectable today. $1,050–1,500 (£700–1,000)

○ **1920 Audemars Piguet produced the smallest minute-repeater watch.**
○ **1920s Audemars Piguet made watch movements for New York's famous jewellery firm Tiffany & Co.**
○ **1922 The first self-winding wristwatch was produced**
○ **1921 Ralco produced one of the (if not the) earliest split-second chronographs.**
○ **1924 John Harwood patented his design for the first automatic wristwatch in England, and in Switzerland in 1926 found a manufacturer to make it.**
○ **1926 The Swiss company Ebauches SA was formed.**
○ **1927 The first perpetual calendar wristwatch was produced by Patek Philippe.**
○ **1927 The first water-resistant watch – the Rolex Oyster – was produced and one was worn by Mercedes Gleitz when she swam the English Channel that year.**
○ **1928 The American watch firm Hamilton made its Piping Rock wristwatch, which became very popular in this period.**
○ **1929 The English firm Dunhill launched its first wristwatch.**

1930s

Despite the economic gloom after the Wall Street Crash in the USA in 1929, and the growing menace of fascism in Europe, there was still a quest for fun among the more well-off in society. The desire for travel also became even more prevalent as the means of doing it got even faster.

By this time wristwatches were accounting for over a third of the watch market. Some cases and dials were enamelled in the Art Deco style, which still pervaded fashion on both sides of the Atlantic. The American watch company Hamilton produced watches with enamelled bezels, such as the Coronado and Piping Rock. (Damage to such enamel bezels will affect their value today.) Watches were also being designed to suit a particular activity, such as Jaeger-LeCoultre's Reverso for sportsmen, which was launched in 1931. Its case pivots through a 180-degree turn so that during any strenuous activity the watch and dial are safe from accidental damage. Rolex built upon the success of its Oyster watch by introducing the Rolex Oyster Perpetual in 1930, which was both waterproof and fitted with an automatic mechanism. Indeed, it was a decade that saw the popularity of the chronograph wristwatch rise to new heights.

The advent of the Talkies in 1927 meant that there was an increase in the number of cinemas. These splendid temples, often in the prevailing Art Deco style, provided a welcome means of escape for the population at large who could leave their everyday lives behind to experience all the glamour of the period. It marked what was the beginning of a long association in the public mind between advertisers of certain brands of wristwatches and the stars who wore them. In 1932 the film actress Joan Crawford promoted a Rolls design automatic wristwatch for the prestigious Swiss firm Blancpain.

At the beginning of this period Mido produced a number of watches based on the radiator designs of cars such as the Bugatti. Many of these were done in agreement with associations of car owners. These novelty watches were probably worn by the car owners to indicate that they were wealthy enough to own such a car.

This decade was also the period when the gem-set cocktail watch appeared (*see page 90*). Beautiful gold-and-enamel watches on chains were still made during the Art Deco era and can be found in round, oval, and ball shapes. Not all ladies' watches were made to be worn on the wrist. The purse watch, as its name suggests, was especially designed to be carried in a purse or handbag and elegant examples survive from this period.

Ingersoll, a firm with American origins, started to produce character watches, such as the Mickey Mouse watch. Included among these designs was a pocket watch and wristwatch for Scouts, the paper dial of which bore the various "virtues" and ideals while the hour hand had "BE PREPARED" on it and the minute hand inscribed "A SCOUT IS".

◀ A 9-carat gold Rolex Oyster octagonal wristwatch, 1931. The Oyster was the first waterproof wristwatch with a screwed down back and winding crown. The crown is a later replacement. The gold case of this example, with applied Arabic numerals and a milled bezel, bears a 1931 import mark for Glasgow. The mark shows that the gold case met British hallmarking standards. $1,800–2,250 (£1,200–1,500)

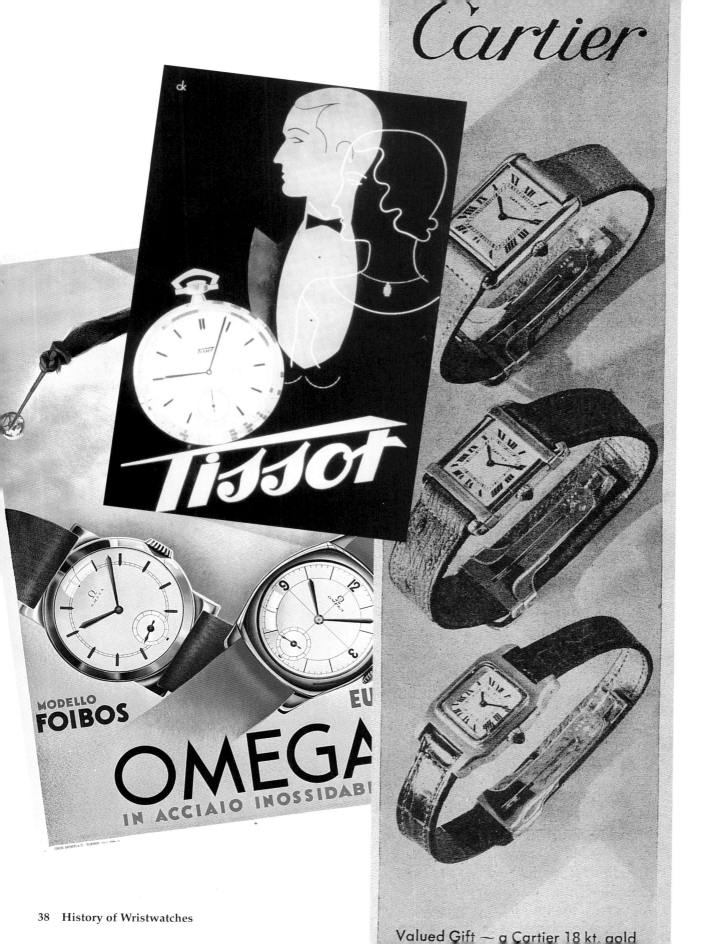

► Rectangular Gruen *c.*1930. This large watchcase is made in two tones of gold. The main part is in white gold while the top and bottom of the case is in ribbed yellow gold. It is not unusual to find watches in coloured gold other than yellow, and even in a combination of two colours. The dial has applied Breguet-style numerals. $3,000–4,500 (£2,000–3,000)

► 1930s rectangular Omega dated *c.*1935. The good condition of the two-tone silver and gilt dial is a plus for collectors. The rectangular shape of both the case and dial is very typical of the Art Deco period, as is the use of the square subsidiary seconds dial. This watch also has a fine crocodile strap. $4,500–7,500 (£3,000–5,000)

◄ The Patek Calatrava remains one of Patek Philippe's most popular models. Its name comes from the Calatrava Cross, which is the emblem Patek Philippe adopted as a symbol. $4,500–7,500 (£3,000–5,000)

◄ The Rolex Prince watch is highly collectable if in good condition. The flared design is a lovely feature of the period and this example has a striped dial. Watches with subsidiary dials like this are often known as doctors' watches, as having the seconds hand separate from the other hands makes taking a pulse count much easier. $7,500–10,500 (£5,000–7,000)

○ **1930 The baguette-shaped movement, which is the smallest one used for ladies' watches, was introduced.**
○ **1930 Mido produced the Bugatti radiator watch.**
○ **1930 Tissot introduced the first anti-magnetic wristwatch.**
○ **1932 Charles Lindbergh's watch design was first produced commercially by Longines.**

○ **1932 Omega became the official timekeepers at the Los Angeles Olympic Games.**
○ **1932 Rolex patented the first automatic wristwatch mechanism with a fully rotating weight (rotor).**
○ **1933 Ingersoll's Mickey Mouse watch was made for children.**
○ **1933 Incabloc shock protection system was first introduced. This**

system ensured the constant time-keeping of a watch (*see* page 26).
○ **1936 Breitling introduced the first chronograph wristwatch with two buttons.**
○ **1937 First world timer wrist-watch was made (*see* page 26).**
○ **1938 Rolex produced its Bubble Back automatic wristwatch, so-called because of the curved back of the case.**

1940s

Sadly "the war to end all wars" had not proved to be so. In 1939 Europe was plunged into war once more to fight against the evils of fascism and in 1941 the Japanese attack on Pearl Harbor meant that the USA also got involved. In Europe the war enveloped most countries and, even when peace came, the cost meant that there was a period of austerity.

World War II caused watch manufacturers on both sides of the Atlantic to produce watches for use by the armed forces. These military watches influenced designs for other men's watches, which were now larger in size and less effeminate than those from previous decades. Switzerland was still a neutral country, which meant that its watch manufacturers could produce military watches such as the Mido Multifort, which was designed to withstand most world climates, whether hot or cold, humid or dry, while also being able to continue with the development of new watch techniques. Patek Philippe was able to introduce the first chronograph wristwatch with a perpetual calendar in 1941 and in 1947 the Cricket, the first mass-produced wristwatch alarm, was launched

by Vulcain. It is worth noting that by the beginning of the decade the making of wristwatches accounted for over 90 per cent of the Swiss watch and clock industry. By the end of the 1940s there was a move away from rectangular watch shapes and an increased use of square models.

One of the great post-war adventures was Thor Heyerdahl's famous voyage across the Pacific on his balsa-wood raft *Kon-Tiki*, which in 1947 brought the Swiss firm of Eterna enduring fame. They had made and supplied Heyerdahl and all his crew with a hardwearing, waterproof watch – the KonTiki Eterna – a name that is still kept alive in new models today.

A story that starts in the late 1940s is that of the American designer Nathan George Horwitt, who sought to create a simple watch dial without the numerals or batons found on most dials. His design style was influenced by the Bauhaus Movement and the resulting watch was a masterpiece of simplicity – its black dial having a golden dot at the 12 o'clock position and simple tapering golden hands. The rest of this story belongs to the early 1960s (*see* page 46).

▶ Omega Royal Air Force wristwatch, 1941. The Royal Air Force ordered steel-cased waterproof wristwatches from Omega during World War II. $900–1,200 (£600–800)

▲ Glashutte Tutima, military chronograph, *c.*1940. Glashutte is the watchmaking town in Germany. This model, called the Tutima, was issued to the Luftwaffe. Production ceased after World War II. $1,500–2,250 (£1,000–1,500)

▶ Rolex Chronograph. This chronograph has tachometer and telemeter scales and a 30-minute counter. The dial is in perfect condition – a factor that adds value. $6,000–7,500 (£4,000–5,000)

ASED OCT. 1 | The New Gruen Pan American!

nous aviat...

ch chosen official ti...
n. Treasured by air...
me out of the war. I...
w air-world time w...
d forces for this m...
rican watches has b...
be released to civili...

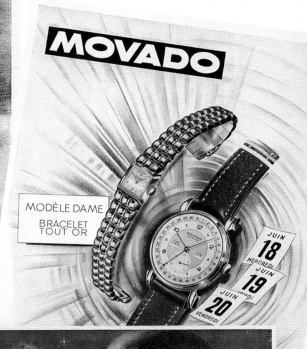

MOVADO

MODÈLE DAME
BRACELET TOUT OR

EL RELOJ SEGURO para el dep...

Seguridades que brinda el TISSOT AQUASPORT para la vida moderna

- **ANTIMAGNETICO**
  Insensible a las irradiaciones electromagnéticas.
- **INOXIDABLE**
  Acero a prueba de corrosión.
- **HERMETICO**
  A prueba de agua y polvo.
- **"SHOCK-ABSORBER"**
  Amortiguador de golpes.
- **CRISTAL IRROMPIBLE**
  Ideal para el deporte.

Y además... PROTEGIDO
CONTRA ACCIDENTES!

Tissot

Científicamente Antimagnético.

POLIZA DE PROTECCION

GARANTIA UNICA EN LA ARGENTINA

Cada TISSOT está munido de una POLIZA DE PROTECCION, que lo cubre por un año contra todo...

6445 - "Aquasport" segundero normal acero $ 145.-
8327 - Para dame...

PASSED BY CENSOR

"Tonight I leaned across 10,000 miles and kissed you!"

This will be a Christmas — more than any other Christmas — which will call for the reassurance of human faith and understanding, for the remembrance of the sympathy and affection human hearts can hold for each other. Is there at this time any gift you could make to a loved one — half the world away, or close at home — more meaningful than a truly fine watch?

Realize, this Christmas, that when you choose a Gruen you choose a watch whose faithful accuracy is the heritage of a highly skilled craftsmanship that goes back nearly seventy years. Your Gruen jeweler has the lovely new models now on display. Every one of them such a triumph of exquisite design it is easy to understand why

America's leading fashion experts call Gruen "America's best-styled watch." Why not see the new models and make your Christmas selection today? Gruen watches, at Gruen jewelers only, from $24.75 to $250; with precious stones to $4,000. Prices include Federal Tax.

Write for free folder "W." The Gruen Watch Company, Time Hill, Cincinnati, Ohio, U. S. A. In Canada, Toronto, Ontario.
Gruen continues to manufacture only such quantities of watches as will not interfere with our aid to our Government in the war program.

A. VER-THIN LEXINGTON...
B. VERI-THIN CARLTON...
C. VERI-THIN MADISON...
D. VERI-THIN GRACE...
E. VERI-THIN VOGUE...
F. ARCADIA...

GRUEN...MAKERS OF THE PRECISION WATCH...AND PRECISION INSTRUMENTS FOR WAR

GRUEN
THE PRECISION WATCH

BUY A GRUEN WATCH
BUT NOT A WAR BOND FIRST!

▶ The Eterna is a typical watch of the 1940s – its teardrop lugs are particularly indicative of the decade. Its clear dial, with Arabic numerals, has ensured its lasting popularity – it is a model that is still produced today. $1,125–2,250 (£750–1,500)

▶ IWC Mark X. This was developed as a military watch. The black dial provides the perfect foil for reading the large, luminous numerals and hands. This watch was superseded in 1948 by the Mark XI (*see* page 78). $1,500–2,250 (£1,000–1,500)

◀ Omega black-dial chronograph. Once again this watch has the classic military styling – large luminous figures and hands on a black ground, for easy reading. It also has a 30-minute counter. Omega provided watches for the armed forces during, and since, the last world war. $1,500–1,250 (£1,000–1,500)

◀ Universal Tri Compax. This stylish chronograph has a moonphase, full calendar, and subsidiary dials for minute and hour recording and constant seconds. The outer scale is a tachometer. It is regarded as the first mass-produced complication. This model is still in production today, although many collector's prefer the design of the earlier cases. $3,000–3,750 (£2,000–2,500)

○ **1941** The first chronograph watch with a perpetual calendar was launched by Patek Philippe.
○ **1943** The launch of manually wound chronograph wrist-watches with an ordinary calendar function.
○ **1945** Rolex introduced its DateJust, which was the first wristwatch to show the date on its dial.

○ **1946** The thinnest watch movement (1.64mm) was produced and used by both Vacheron & Constantin and Audemars Piguet.
○ **1946** First mass-produced alarm wristwatch made by Vulcain.
○ **1947** Omega launched a 7.5 minute tourbillon wristwatch – the button for setting the hands was situated at 4 o'clock.

○ **1947** Jaeger-LeCoultre introduced a gold automatic wristwatch with a power-reserve indicator on the dial.
○**1948** IWC produced the Mark XI, an anti-magnetic chronograph. This is an eagerly sought-after military watch today (*see* page 79).
○ **1949** Heuer introduced its Solunar wristwatch, which featured a tidal indicator.

1950s

By the early 1950s there was a growing sense of optimism, reflecting the change to the old order of society brought about through World War II. The Festival of Britain in 1951 saw the advent of new designs that reflected the growing interest in technology and science, and the accession of Queen Elizabeth II heralded what was felt to be a new Elizabethan Age.

However, this was not reflected in the world of wristwatches. Although everyone wanted to own one, prices were still relatively high and advertising was still aimed at the maturer end of the market. Designs for both men's and ladies' watches focused mainly on simple round designs for both, with ladies' models being quite small in size. Automatic watches were particularly popular.

While designs did not change much for most of the decade, several watches made during this time caught the public's imagination. In 1953 Blancpain produced the Fifty Fathoms water-resistant watch, which could be worn to a depth of 656ft (200m). Jacques Cousteau, the French oceanographer, and his crew made the film

Silent World in 1956; in it they were wearing Fifty Fathom watches, which helped to make the watch a success. Activities in the skies were not neglected either. Breitling introduced its Navitimer in 1952. This watch was aimed specifically at pilots since its chronograph movement allowed them to use it to check their flight plans, speed, and fuel consumption. The Speedmaster Professional chronograph was then launched by Omega in 1956 and, as its name suggests, was aimed initially at sportsmen. However, it was in succeeding decades that it would achieve its greatest fame as being the watch favoured by NASA for their astronauts.

There were many technical developments at this time, such as the creation of the first battery-driven watch by the Frenchman Fred Lip, who worked with American firm Elgin on the project. (It would be another American company, Hamilton, that would succeed with a commercially viable electronic watch – the Ventura 500 in 1957.) The concept certainly struck a chord with the consumer society of the day, and further developments eventually led to the quartz watch.

◄ A 9-carat gold Rolex gentleman's wristwatch, 1954. This manually wound watch, which has a circular dial with applied numerals and centre seconds hand, is very much a classic look for the 1950s.
$1,200–1,800 (£800–1,200)

▲ A gilt, base-metal bangle watch, Marcel Boucher, 1950s. This very stylish ladies' watch encapsulates the fashions of the decade. It is a digital watch in which the hours and minutes are marked on rotating discs. While not of great value, it is collectable as a style/fashion item and has survived in good condition with little wear to the gilded finish.
$1,125–2,250 (£750–1,500)

► Omega "Pie-Pan" Constellation. This was introduced in 1952 and, although redesigned later, remains one of Omega's most popular designs. The distinctive dial and batons of the original encapsulate '50s design. This version is called "Grand Lux" and came in a sterling silver box. It is regarded by collectors as the most desirable of all Constellations. $4,500–7,500 (£3,000–5,000)

► Hamilton Ventura, 1957. This, the first electrical watch (*see* page 104), was designed by Richard Arbib, who designed cars and other 1950s items. It was the first time Hamilton had used an outside designer. $3,000–3,750 (£2,000–2,500)

◄ Omega Cosmic Square Moonphase. This marvellous classic gold gentleman's watch has it all: elegant square case design with extended lugs, moonphase, and calendar with day and month apertures. $4,500–7,500 (£3,000–5,000)

◄ The Breitling Navitimer was first introduced in 1952 and has remained one of Breitling's most popular models. It has special features for aircraft pilots, including a slide-rule function on the outer side of the dial, which allows the pilot to calculate speed and fuel consumption as well as check flight plans. $1,800–2,700 (£1,200–1,800)

○ 1951 Movado launched its World Time model, the Polygraph, at the Basle Fair.
○ 1952 The Constellation, one of Omega's most enduring models, was introduced.
○ 1952 Fred Lip and Elgin work on the first prototypes for the first battery-driven watch.
○ 1953 Tissot's Navigator was introduced – the first automatic World Time watch with a calendar.
○ 1953 Sir Edmund Hillary conquered Everest while wearing a Rolex Explorer.
○ 1955 Vacheron Constantin produced, at that time, the world's thinnest watch in celebration of the firm's centenary.
○ 1956 The Parashock was launched by the Japanese firm Citizen. It was the first Japanese shockproof wristwatch.
○ 1956 Jaeger-LeCoultre produced the Memovox, the first automatic wristwatch to have an alarm.
○ 1958 Gruen in the USA launched its Super-G, which has jumping hours (*see* p154).
○ 1958 Golden Voice, the first ladies' wristwatch with an alarm, was launched by Vulcain.

1960s

The story of Horwitt's watch, which started on page 40, can be finished here. Horwitt, who patented the design in 1958, was unable to find any watch manufacturer to take up his idea. The design was then incorporated into the permanent collection of the Museum of Modern Art in New York and in 1961 Movado bought the rights to it, launching what became known as the Museum Watch.

The 1960s was an era of great social change, especially for the younger generation. Musical phenomenons such as The Beatles and The Rolling Stones revolutionized the way young people behaved, and the youth of society soon became an important part of the consumer market.

The 1960s also saw watch designs change to a much heavier, larger look for both men and women. The small-sized ladies' watch became a thing of the past. There was a move, towards the end of the decade, to produce watches with coloured dials, often incorporating real semi-precious stones such as tiger's-eye or lapis lazuli. Piaget was one of the leading exponents of this trend. Many of the models were bracelet watches, in either yellow or white-gold, and

watches made for evening wear may well have a diamond-set bezel around the dial. Even the renowned firm of Patek Philippe joined in, making the Ellipse – a stylish asymmetrical watch – in 1969. Such watches really reflect the era they were produced in, and here the world of watch-collecting overlaps with that of design.

The American firm Bulova invented the Accutron – a watch regulated by a tuning fork, which vibrated at 360Hz. This meant that the firm could guarantee that there would not be monthly variation of more than a minute. The model was produced until 1976, but of course the advent of quartz meant that the days of the electro-mechanical watch were numbered.

The decade also saw the continuing development of battery-powered watches. In 1966 a Swiss firm produced Beta 1, the first movement using a quartz oscillator, and two years later both Switzerland and Japan had developed prototypes that were launched officially in 1969. The design of these early quartz watches was rather clumsy. Many had either LCD or LED displays rather than the more usual analogue design. It would take further developments for a more "normal" look to be achieved.

▲ A Heuer Autavia GMT chronograph, *c.*1965. This manual-wind chronograph has a 12-hour indicator as well as a second hand for reading different time zones – a reflection perhaps of the growth in world travel during the 1960s. $1,200–2,250 (£800–1,500)

◄ What greater location for an advertisement could you ask for than the moon?! This emphasizes the relationship Omega have had with NASA since the Speedmaster was chosen by NASA as their official chronograph in 1965. And how successful a partnership it has been – when Apollo 13's timing equipment was destroyed the astronauts had to rely on their Speedmasters to return them safely to Earth.

Heuer introduces a $170 chronograph and two less expensive models.

Heuer is known around racing circles for having the most complete line of stopwatches and chronographs going (118 models in all).

So you know when we introduce three new chronographs they must be pretty special.

The 11.404 (left). This Heuer chronograph is a real handful. In fact, it's about 25% larger than a standard stopwatch. And it does a lot more. The 11.404 is a ⅕ of a second recorder that can register elapsed time up to 12 hours. With a 30-minute register for shorter times. It has the split action feature for timing more than one event or sequence at a time.

And it can do what an ordinary stopwatch can never do. It can tell you the time of day. The 11.404 has a 17-jewel precision movement and is protected against shocks.

The Camaro 45 (center). The Camaro is the newest shape in wrist chronographs. We call it the new "square" look. Drivers will find it useful both on and off the track. It's not just a wristwatch, but a precise ⅕ second stopwatch, too. With a register that

records time from zero to 45 minutes. A rugged stainless steel case and a 17-jewel movement equipped with Incabloc shock absorbers. The Camaro 45 is shock-resistant, anti-magnetic and water-proof (as long as crystal, case, crown and push pieces are intact).

You don't have to race or rally to find this Heuer chronograph helpful. You can use it to time just about anything. Your long distance phone calls. Your speeches, Polaroid shots, the time left

in parking meters. Or, if you have a boat, you can use it to time speed runs.

The GMT Master Time (right). This Heuer timer fits the trend started by rallyists around the world and adapted for rally events everywhere. It uses the 24-hour system of recording time. The GMT Master Time is an 8-day precision clock for your dashboard that lets you read Greenwich Mean Time directly without having to add or subtract. It has a hack feature that lets you synchronize the sweep-second and hour hands with official time signals. And if you set all three hands at "24", you can read elapsed time.

The GMT Master Time has a turning bezel with a luminous pointer for setting any known time mark. Its 15-jewel movement is protected against shocks and vibrations.

You can buy Heuer timers at jewelry and specialty stores and at sports car accessory shops.

For our new catalog, send 25¢ to Heuer Time Corp., Dept. 602, 135 E. 44 St., N.Y. N.Y. 10017. (212) OX 7-2150.

11.404 chronograph: $170.

Camaro 45 $69.50.

GMT Master Time: $62.50.

▶ The Heuer Carrera chronograph was launched in 1963. It has a 45-minute counter and a tachometer (*see* page 130). $1,800–3,000 (£1,200–2,000)

▶ Zenith El Primero. The automatic chronograph movement El Primero was first launched in 1969 and sold well during the early 1970s (*see* page 70). It is powered by a central winding rotor and its stopwatch function is able to record times to the nearest 10th of a second. $1,350–2,250 (£900–1,500)

◀ Omega Speedmaster Moonwatch. This was first created in 1956 as a sports chronograph but its use by NASA has led to it being given the nickname "Moonwatch", and it has become highly sought-after by collectors. $1,200–2,625 (£800–1,750)

◀ Bulova Accutron Spaceview, c.1965. The name of this watch reflects the interest in space travel and the fact that the electro-mechanical workings of this watch, including the tuning fork, can be seen clearly. $375–750 (£250–500)

○ **1960** The American Bulova Accutron, which uses an electric tuning fork and was invented by Max Hetzel, first came onto the market.
○ **1962** Eterna introduced the Eterna-Matic 3000, which was the thinnest automatic men's and ladies' wristwatch.
○ **1964** Seiko acted as time-keeper at the Tokyo Olympics in its home country of Japan.
○ **1966 The first mechanical wristwatch with a high-frequency movement – the balance vibrates 36,000 times an hour – was introduced by Girard-Perregaux.**
○ **1969 Girard-Perregaux developed the first mass-produced quartz watch.**
○ **1969 Longines produced** the first quartz cybernetic wristwatch, which was a quartz watch that did not have an integrated circuit.
○ **1969 Neil Armstrong wore an Omega Speedmaster when landing on the moon.**
○ **1969 The Dynamic, an oval wristwatch with a broad, brightly coloured strap, was launched by Omega.**

1970s

The social changes of the 1960s carried on into the 1970s – the younger market was definitely here to stay. If design in the 1960s had in some cases looked back to Art Nouveau, there was now a return to the more geometric shapes seen in Art Deco. For some it was a time of excess, especially for followers of Punk and Glam Rock, and by the start of the 1980s there was a move towards more traditional ways and fashions.

The introduction of the quartz movement wristwatch in 1968 brought many changes in the global watch industry. These included a rise, during the first part of the 1970s, of bulky watches using either liquid crystal display or light-emitting diodes (LCD or LED), before public opinion resulted in a move back to more conventional watch forms. The successful emergence of Japanese watch manufacturers into the world market led to a period of mergers, closures, and takeovers among Swiss watch manufacturers and sadly the records of many of these firms were destroyed or lost.

Consumerism was increasing too, and it was a period that saw the beginning of a designer-label consciousness among shoppers. This encouraged designers and firms like Yves Saint Laurent and Christian Dior to have watches made with dials bearing their logo or name. Many of these watches were produced by Swiss manufacturers. One notable design is Chopard's Happy Diamonds wristwatch, which the company first introduced in 1976. It is so-called because of the seven gold-collared diamonds that move around the dial through the wearer's wrist movement. The Geneva-based firm Raymond Weil was successfully launched in 1976 and many of the extra-slim watches produced have had names that reflect the Weil's interest in opera. The watch manufacturer Corum produced a series of designs that encapsulate the taste of the period, such as its Rolls-Royce grille watch, which has the Spirit of Ecstasy forming part of the watch's 12 o'clock lug, and their ingot watch, which is made of a small gold or platinum ingot.

The watch known as the Buckingham, made by Corum, was a classic piece of 1970s design with its generious case size. They were made originally in 18-carat gold only, but today they have been re-released in a stainsteel case, with a peacock tail-feather as the dial of the watch.

◀ Heuer Autavia Chronograph, c.1972. This watch uses Heuer's first self-winding chronograph movement. It also has an outer bezel with tachometer markings. $1,125–1,500 (£750–1,000)

▲ The Omega Geneve Dynamic, which at one time became Omega's best-selling watch. The design was the same for ladies' and men's watches. $300–450 (£200–300)

The Omega Dynamic
...first watch

(female)

on the pores of your skin. The strap
made of Corfam. It looks and feels
other but takes to the water like a duck.
re are self-winding and hand-wound
nics. The choice is yours.

How can a man in a $27,000 suit settle for a $235 watch?

The Apollo-Soyuz spacesuits, like those for every preceding space mission, were designed especially for the job. Not surprising either. You'd hardly expect to find the equipment for the flight through space to this historic America-Russia meeting ready-invented in the shops.

Yet that's how the astronauts found the Omega Speedmaster, their watch.

In 1965 NASA picked up a Speedmaster, as simply as you do in your local jewellery shop. And they made it standard flight equipment for every astronaut because, unlike any other chronograph tested, whatever NASA did to the Speedmaster, it stood up.

If you're wearing an Omega Speedmaster you can be proud of it – numerous space missions, six moon landings, and now, almost unbelievably, America and Russia together. For any other watch, the shock would be too much.

1. *Omega Speedmaster Professional Chronograph.*
Standard issue to the American astronauts.
2. *Omega Speedmaster 125. Officially certified*
automatic chronograph chronometer.
3. *Omega Speedsonic f300. Officially certified*
electronic chronograph chronometer.

Ω OMEGA

2572

▼ Omega Megaquartz 2400, 1974. This was the first high-frequency quartz watch and was advertised as the world's most accurate watch. The calibre 1511 version is very special since it was awarded the status of being a marine chronometer (*see* page 122). $1,125–2,250 (£750–1,500)

▲ The Rado Diastar was launched as a scratch-resistant watch in the 1960s but became a 1970s icon. Its distinctive case style and faceted crystal appeal to collectors. $450–900 (£300–600)

► Heuer Monaco Steve McQueen. Film star Steve McQueen was a motor-racing enthusiast and wore this Heuer in the film *Le Mans* (*see* page 132). The watch's square shape is a feature collectors will like, as most chronographs are round. $3,000–4,500 (£2,000–3,000)

► Cartier Santos. This elegant gold and steel wristwatch, introduced in 1978, is a version of the watch first produced by Cartier in the early 1900s. $3,000–4,500 (£2,000–3,000)

❍ 1972 Audemars Piguet produced the first luxury stainless-steel wristwatch, The Royal Oak.
❍ 1972 Longines launched a watch with an LCD display rather than a traditional dial.
❍ 1973 The James Bond movie *Live and Let Die* included a very versatile Rolex as one of Bond's accessories.

❍ 1975 The Heuer Chronosplit, with both LCD and LED functions, was the first quartz chronograph wristwatch.
❍ 1975 Quartz watches for women became feasible with the development of even smaller quartz oscillators.
❍ 1976 A thin quartz movement was introduced by Piaget.
❍ 1978 Vacheron Constantin

produced the gold-and-diamond-set Kallista bracelet watch, which sold for $5 million (£3.3 million).
❍ 1978 IWC's compass watch was designed by Ferdinand Porsche.
❍ 1979 A very flat quartz movement, the Delirium, was launched by Swiss company SMH as a response to Japanese dominance of the market.

1980s to Present Day

It may seem strange that with the continuing growth in the quartz market during the 1980s and '90s, and into the new millennium, the interest and demand for mechanical watches has not disappeared but rather grown into a collector's market. Certainly the quartz watch revolution continues. The introduction of small quartz movements has allowed manufacturers to produce designs such as the cufflink watch, where each link can be set to different time zones. The emergence of Swatch in the 1980s appealed to younger generations and their innovative designs and special editions have attracted a huge number of collectors around the world. In the early 1990s there was a tremendous interest among young people in the huge range of watches that were exported from Russia for the Western market. Children are well catered for with novelty watches that have been created for them by the firm Flik-Flak since the late 1980s – some of these can even be machine-washed.

In a move that perhaps reflects public interest in the unusual, Tissot launched their Rock Watch in 1985. Each example is unique because it is made out of Swiss granite, so no two watches can ever be the same. The company followed this up with a series of watches, including one made from wood and others whose dials were made from coral, mother-of-pearl, and other natural materials. Corum produced the Météorite watch in the late 1980s, which has a dial made up from slices of a meteorite that crashed into Greenland; each dial, of course, is unique.

It should not be a surprise that Andy Warhol, who said everyone has their 15 minutes of fame, should have been a collector of watches (a fact revealed following his death in 1987) as one of the last things that Warhol designed was a bracelet watch for Movado. Made up of five watch-faces linked together, each face has a photographic view of New York that serves as the dial.

▼ Panerai Divers' watch. The Panerai company of Italy made watches for the Italian navy frogmen in World War II. The design has not altered, and a much newer version, from 2003, is shown here. $3,750–5,250 (£2,500–3,500)

▲ This 2003 watch by Franck Muller has a distinctive dial based on the wheels of a gaming table; it is inspired by the tonneau-shaped watches of the 1920s. $15,000–22,500 (£10,000–15,000)

▲ Cartier Tank Française, 1996. From the 1980s Cartier have relaunched their famous Tank model with slight variations in design (*see* pp56–57). $4,500–6,000 (£3,000–4,000)

► Tissot T Touch. This is one of the latest designs around. It is a multi-functional watch – to select what you want you touch the glass in the appropriate place, rather than pressing a button (*see page 24*). $510–555 (£340–370)

► Cartier Roadster. This distinctively shaped automatic watch has an unusual dial decoration that was inspired by the dashboard clocks from the cars of the 1950s Hense Roadster. $3,300–4,350 (£2,200–2,900)

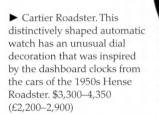

◄ Alan Silberstein Krono. The 1990s saw a rise in the number of "art watches" produced. Alan Silberstein is a well-known French architect who now has his own watchmaking company. The design of this chronograph was based on the Bauhaus style. $7,500–15,000 (£5,000–10,000)

◄ Ulysse Nardin Freak. This has a unique movement that rotates to tell the time without using conventional hands. The time is set by rotating the bezel. $33,000–42,000 (£22,000–28,000)

○ 1983 Swatch watch brand launched in Britain, Germany, and Switzerland.
○ 1983 Rolex Sea Dweller was launched – it can be used underwater to a depth of 4,000 ft (1,220m).
○ 1985 The launch of the TAG Heuer brand.
○ 1987 The Tissot Two-Timer came on the market – it tells the time through both analogue and digital display.
○ 1991 Blancpain introduced the most complicated wristwatch – the 1735 – an automatic, split-seconds, minute-repeating chronograph with perpetual calendar and tourbillon escapement.
○ 1996 The Patek Philippe Museum paid in excess of SF2,000,000 ($1,218,300) for one of its minute-repeating wristwatches with perpetual calendar.
○ 1998 The first ladies' minute-repeating wristwatch with carillon was launched by Audemars Piguet.
○ 1999 Girard-Perregaux introduced an automatic chronograph with a flying-seconds hand capable of timing to an eighth of a second.

How to Compare
and Value

Rectangular Watches I

It seems likely that no one made rectangular timepieces before the advent of the wristwatch – at least not in any quantity – so rectangular cases have an important place in history as they emphasize the fact that these first wristwatches were not just small pocket watches with straps attached.

Cartier's Tank design is important for many other reasons too. It is actually one of the most famous and recognized watch designs of all. The legend, as espoused not least by Cartier, is that both design and name derive from the first tanks deployed in Flanders during World War I. There are some drawings surviving that show the rationale behind the creation of the Tank. The design is so simple as to nearly defy definition – there is simply nothing that detracts from the essential design and the proportions work perfectly. The Tank was also one of the first rectangular watches to be made in any number and, effectively, it laid down the ground rules for the treatment of dials and hands in such watches. The first Tank watches pioneered some of the distinguishing features of early wristwatch designs, such as the "sword" hands and "railway tracks" to show the minutes. There are few watches that you can say belong in every collection but the Cartier Tank, in one of its many incarnations, is perhaps the only watch whose place is universally accepted.

Hamilton are, of course, one of the USA's most famous watch houses and one of the few American companies whose wristwatches are widely sought after by collectors, particularly in the USA. Hamilton produced on an industrial scale for much of the market, and gained a good reputation for both wristwatches and pocket watches – particularly for the reliability of the watches with which they supplied railroad companies.

The Cambridge, and similar models such as the Ardmore, Wilshire, and Brock, were made in the 1930s and 1940s. Mostly in steel, there were also examples in gold or gold-filled cases, and a few, rare, platinum ones.

Hamilton Cambridge, late 1940s

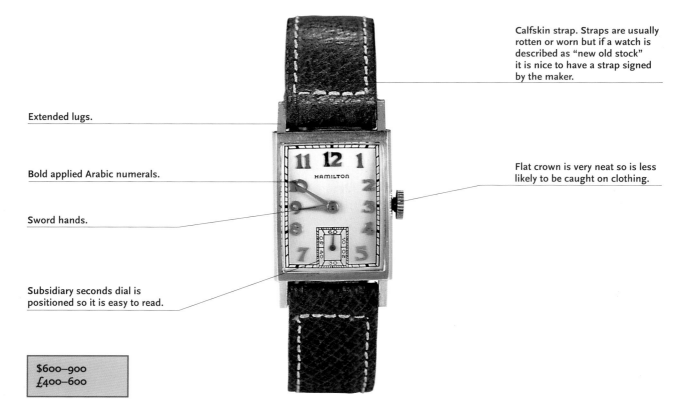

Calfskin strap. Straps are usually rotten or worn but if a watch is described as "new old stock" it is nice to have a strap signed by the maker.

Extended lugs.

Bold applied Arabic numerals.

Sword hands.

Subsidiary seconds dial is positioned so it is easy to read.

Flat crown is very neat so is less likely to be caught on clothing.

$600–900
£400–600

Modern Cartier Tank, 1980s

Crocodile strap with deployant clasp. This clasp ensures the watch can't drop off the wrist, and reduces wear on the strap by as much as two years.

Guilloch-patterned dial with Roman numerals.

Winding crown set with a cabouchon sapphire, which is a Cartier tradition.

Note the original Tank design's extended bars, which serve to provide a little extra protection to the case. These actually echo the shape of the military tanks' tracks.

Faceted crystal glass. Always check this for wear and tear as it may be chipped.

$3,500–3,750
£2,000–2,500

▼ The enduring nature of the original Tank's design is shown by how close the modern version is to the original. One of the most pleasing aspects to have become part of the established design is the engine-turned dial decoration, which has become as much a hallmark as the case shape. Highlighted below is the secret Cartier signature that every Tank now incorporates as a defence against counterfeiting – unsurprisingly the Tank is a staple of the faker's business.

• *There are a few drawbacks to rectangular cases that collectors should bear in mind. The main one is that they are comparatively fragile – at least compared to round-case watches. Corners are not only more prone to shocks, but they are more difficult to proof satisfactorily against the elements. A consequence of this is that rectangular cases have always tended to be more expensive to produce – a truth even today. Although the possibility of wear should not be a huge consideration for the collector, nevertheless a little extra attention paid to the condition of rectangular watches is probably justified.*

How the Tank Evolved

The "Tank" was designed in 1917 by Louis Cartier and was named after and inspired by the tanks that, along with American entry into World War I, finally brought the conflict to a close. Juxtaposition of the watch and a top view of the early tanks makes the derivation clear. However, the longevity of the Tank is based on more than a passing resemblance to military machinery. The simplicity and proportions of the watch are the reasons for its success.

It could be argued that the Tank (and the Santos, another famed rectangular watch from Cartier) epitomize everything that made Cartier's venture into watchmaking such a great success.

Louis François Cartier founded the company in 1847, when it quickly became a favourite of the Imperial Court, and the focus was almost entirely on jewellery. It was not until 1898 that a link with Cartier's future in watch-making was made. In that year the founder's grandson, Louis Cartier, joined the family firm and injected new life into the company almost immediately by his cultivation of the most glamorous and well-heeled people of the day as key clientele – including Edward, the then Prince of Wales.

Rectangular Watches II

After World War I the wristwatch had started to become a more attractive form of timepiece than the pocket watch. In the 1920s the Swiss firm Rolex, headed by Hans Wilsdorf, saw the new potential and started to produce some interesting watches. These are now among the most collectable pieces on the market today.

Rectangular watches with Paris or Arabic numerals were very much the style of the time, with fine engine-finished dials that, when light was reflected on them, resembled watered silk cloth. The earlier piece, shown below, represents this well, and this style was used by a lot of other watch companies – Cartier still use the finish today as it ties into the fashionable 1920s look. The Rolex Prince was, and still is, a flamboyant-looking watch, with the tiger-striped case with its two-toned flared sides. Movements had also progressed, with expensive rectangular-shaped pieces rather than

the simpler round-shaped mechanisms that would have a more universal use. The movements on the Prince models were also of a far higher standard and were chronometer checked, which means the movements were tested over a number of days at different temperatures and positions, and this information was written on a certificate. These certificates are sometimes still included with the watch in a compartment at the bottom of the fitted case. This all adds to the value and makes the Prince the most interesting model for collectors worldwide. Later on, in the late 1930s, the watch was fitted with a less expensive oval movement – a model that can be bought at a lesser price due to this fact. The market for rectangular watches is always going to be smaller; they are not waterproof because sealing a square watch is not practical, and round watches have always been more popular in terms of looks.

18ct Gold Rolex, 1920s

The case can suffer from wear at the corners so look out for lead-solder fillers. The case should also have a reference number engraved on the back; check this ties up with the relevant model.

Black-painted Paris or Arabic numerals are very much a 1920s look.

This strap would not be original, but this would not affect the value; it would have been sewn on with fixed bars.

The winding crown may have had the factory logo but these are often changed due to wear.

The glass is originally early unbreakable cellulose, which on unrestored pieces appears yellow; but more often than not the glass has been replaced.

$1,200–1,800
£800–1,200

Rolex Two-Coloured Gold Brancard Prince, 1928

The domed cellulose, or plastic, unbreakable glass can discolour and is often replaced, but this does not affect the value.

The original straps had detachable pins; although this strap is not original this does not affect the overall value.

The dial on this watch is in its original condition and has some evidence of patina; this makes the piece more desirable.

The inner minute track, as opposed to the outer track on the earlier model, is a feature of this particular watch.

A subsidiary running seconds hand appeared on watches as a useful feature but it was also to assure the wearer that the watch was still working.

The brancard, or stretcher, case is the most collectable style with its tiger-striped finish.

$7,500–10,500
£5,000–7,000

• *The Rolex Prince is one of the finest and most sought-after watches. As a result it is often faked – not the movement itself as it would be too expensive to reproduce, but the cases can be reproduced in gold and platinum and can have even the experts fooled. The most difficult cases to fake are those in stainless steel as it is harder to cast.*

• *The name "doctor's watch" is associated with the Rolex Prince, not because doctors bought them but because they were a favourite present from wealthy patients; the separate subsidiary seconds hand could be used for timing pulse rates.*

The Rolex Prince

The Rolex Prince watch was produced from the late 1920s until the late 1930s when a model with a simpler straight-sided case was produced, and this continued to be made right up until the early 1950s.

The Rolex Prince ref 971 is one of the most collectable pieces; the case is engraved on the back and similarly stamped on the inside of the bezel. These pieces were produced in lots of variations, from humble stainless steel to the rarest model in platinum.

The term Brancard is French for stretcher, which is very much what this style of case resembles. The white metal colour was fashionable at the time, and on the silver models the cases were chrome-plated to prevent discolouration. After 70 years this plating can make the watch case look like a fake because the chrome starts to flake off. However, this can be restored to bring back the original look. Stainless steel was also used and such examples are very collectable as they do not seem to have been copied to the same degree as the gold pieces.

The dials can also suffer as the cellulose lacquer breaks down and this can cause the silvering on the dial to turn black. Having an original dial is important and will make the watch more desirable in the future.

Rectangular Watches III

The two watches shown here may look like they have been made from the same material, but one is platinum while the other is steel. Platinum is far more exotic and so worth a great deal more.

The platinum tonneau piece from IWC is a good example of everything a collector might be looking for. It was intended as a prestige model from the outset and benefits from a very high standard of finish, as can be seen from the dial. The watch has a silvered face with applied numerals and the hour markers and hands are all finished to a high standard. The case itself is worth attention; see, for example, the strap lugs that extend, as part of the design, beyond the case. Examine the case closely and you can see the extra complexity of construction that makes the case a functioning part of an interesting design. That the watch is made of platinum means that the surface is durable and virtually impervious to oxidation or tarnishing. IWC has always been one of the more sought-after names. This particular watch was sold at auction complete with all its paperwork – an important bonus point for collectors. It is also simply an attractive watch, far more of its time than the Omega model.

However, it should be said that the Omega watch on this page was never intended to compete with the IWC piece, even though it is of a near-identical vintage. Omega has always been a slightly less exclusive house than IWC – a comparison that still applies today (current perceptions of a brand's value can have an undoubted impact on the value of vintage examples). This particular watch is, nevertheless, an attractive example of its type. Unlike the IWC, the Omega case is simply a functional frame and holder for the design of the dial, which has a basic attraction. However, note that the difference in price owes much to the lack of applied numerals on the Omega model and its having much more basic hands. The case construction is also a simpler affair and somehow has a more dated feel.

Steel Omega, *c.*1930

Welded wire lugs meant that the straps had to be sown onto the watch. This was much safer as straps that are joined to the case can be vulnerable.

Steel case.

Silvered dial in excellent condition, with printed numerals, indices, and minute track. The good condition possibly indicates a restoration or replacement.

Sword-shaped hands.

This flat crown is the most used shape on rectangular watches as it helps to maintain the angular lines.

Watch for damage on exposed corners, as rectangular watches are more susceptible to this.

The subsidiary dial is easy to read.

$450–600
£300–400

IWC Calibre 87, 1938

Expensive watches traditionally have crocodile skin straps to give a luxurious look and feel.

Silvered dial.

"Pomme"-shaped hands, derived from the clock and pocket watch styles, are retro classic in look.

Complex and sophisticated faceted case that is difficult to produce.

The strap lugs extend behind the case, creating an extra dimension to the watch's design.

Platinum applied numerals and hour markers.

Small seconds dial.

$3,750–4,500
£2,500–3,000

• *An accompanying bill of sale and a receipt for service by the maker (as the above watch has) is of great importance to collectors and can raise the value of a watch considerably.*

• *The steel case can be repolished to look like new, but some collectors like the scratches as they indicate the watch's age and authenticity.*

Platinum

Platinum has been prized since its discovery in ancient Egypt. It is a silver-white metal in its pure form and is extremely resistant to chemical attack.

In the late 1800s platinum mania swept through Europe and Russia. Spain's King Charles IV commissioned a platinum room, while others wore gowns woven with platinum thread. Cartier, Fabergé, and Tiffany all used platinum in their legendary designs. The world's most famous diamonds; the Star of Africa, the Hope, and the Koh-I-Noor, are all secured on platinum settings.

Platinum's resistance to chemical attack means that it is very difficult to refine, though the rewards of doing so are high. The stability and strength of platinum means it is in demand for precision instruments and surgical tools, as well as jewellery.

The watchmaking companies at the top end of the market still make limited editions using platinum, while brands such as Cartier and Patek Philippe use the metal regularly. Collectors like platinum because it looks like steel, so only they know how precious their watches truly are.

Automatic Watches I

The idea of a self-winding, or automatic, watch dates back to the end of the 18th century. However, automatic pocket watches had limited success and were produced only in small numbers. These first watches had a winding weight that was rather like a pedometer, moving up and down on the back of the movement when the wearer was walking. More successful watches had a rotor that moved 360° – such rotors are still used today. Early automatic watches were made by just a few fine makers, such as Breguet or Recordon, and are now worth anything in the region of $6,000–150,000 (£4,000–£100,000).

Utilizing this type of mechanism was not tried again until the early 1920s, when the famous company le Roy produced their first automatic watches. Again these were expensive and made only in small numbers. However, they do sometimes appear on the market, and sell for around $12,000–18,000 (£8,000–12,000).

In 1922 the English watchmaker John Harwood really kickstarted the whole automatic watch concept. He began by using an existing movement and adapted it with his own automatic mechanism. The resulting watch went into production – this first model was of the round design shown on the right. It was produced in silver, gold, and gold plate. His second design, the Autowrist (below), was produced to suit the 1930s fashion for rectangular case shapes. This had limited success due to a couple of factors – in the 1930s the world stock market crashed, and there were also technical problems with the watch. Thus the development of the automatic watch was brought to a halt until other manufacturers later took up the challenge. Both of the watches here are of interest to collectors but, as the name Harwood is not so well-known today, their values are not that high. This does mean that a good Harwood collection can be formed at a fairly low cost.

Harwood Autowrist, 1930s

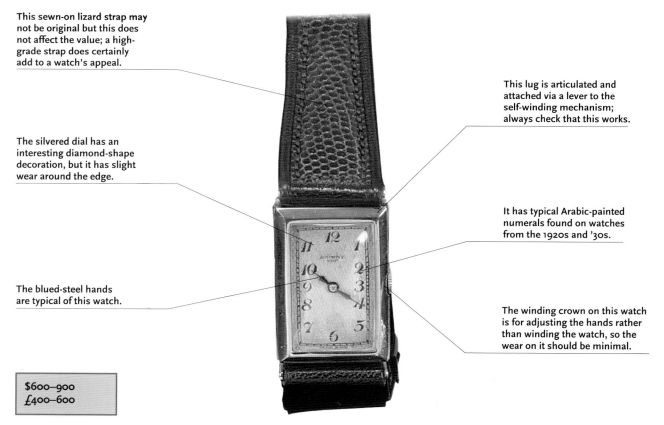

This sewn-on lizard strap may not be original but this does not affect the value; a high-grade strap does certainly add to a watch's appeal.

The silvered dial has an interesting diamond-shape decoration, but it has slight wear around the edge.

The blued-steel hands are typical of this watch.

This lug is articulated and attached via a lever to the self-winding mechanism; always check that this works.

It has typical Arabic-painted numerals found on watches from the 1920s and '30s.

The winding crown on this watch is for adjusting the hands rather than winding the watch, so the wear on it should be minimal.

$600–900
£400–600

Harwood Gold Automatic Wristwatch, 1922

Sewn-on leather strap with fixed bars. These were used only on early watches, before removable pins were invented.

Decorated case lug – check to see if it has had any soft solder repairs.

The blued-steel hands here have pierced elements for luminous paint – make sure that they match.

The silvered dial here shows sign of discolouration due to the lacquer going off.

This red dot indicator showed if the watch had been left in hand set position after being set (done by moving the bezel round). If it had, this would cause problems with the timekeeping.

The milled-edged bezel moves in order to set the hands. You should ensure that this still operates, as there is no winding button on these watches.

$750–1,200
£500–800

- *The Harwood watch was produced in a gold shell case – when you are buying a gold piece check for a hallmark.*

- *Some of the early Harwood watches used fired enamel dials but these are rare and a metal dial is more common.*

- *Engraved case-backs normally decrease the desirability of the watch.*

- *The Autowrist watches were made in smaller numbers so are quite rare today, but this does not mean they are particularly valuable.*

The John Harwood Company

John Harwood was a watch repairer but also an inventor. In his small workshop on the Isle of Man he developed a number of ideas for various automatic mechanisms. He had recognized that there was a general weak spot in watches on the winding button and stem, which could let in dust and dirt that would affect the movement. His idea was to eliminate the winding button completely by creating a watch that didn't need to touched to be set. Through his determination he found English backers who commissioned a Swiss company, Scild, to produce his watch. Unfortunately the interest from other factories was muted as

they did not see any good reason for an automatic timepiece. The company lasted until just 1931, but during that time John Harwood was not discouraged by the lack of interest and problems with his first model. He went on produce the Autowrist, which again wasn't a great success.

There is a wide range of Harwood models, from the gold-plated cased at around $300–450 (£200–300), silver-cased at $450–600 (£300–400), and gold at $750–1,050 (£500–700). These were produced for different markets – for example, in the USA watches were offered with gold-plated cases that had engraved decoration, as this was popular at the time.

Automatic Watches II

With the growing interest in mechanical watches, quartz watches have taken a lesser role. However, the top watch companies have kept the automatic watch alive. Although Harwood may have paved the way initially, it was certainly the more well-known companies that developed the idea further over the years.

The Swiss company Eterna was formed in 1856 by Dr Joseph Gerard and Urs Schild, initially to help with the unemployment in Granges, Canton Solothurn. They began by making pocket watches and then wristwatches, and produced one of the first pocket watches with an alarm. They overcame the problem of the swinging rotor within automatic watches by fitting small steel ballbearings at the rotor axle – these still appear on their dials today. Eterna produced some interesting watches that can be bought for as little $300–450 (£200–300). The firm has changed hands in recent years and is now owned by the company that produces Porsche's designer watches.

Probably one of the most famous watch houses, Patek Philippe was started by Antoine Norbert de Patek. A Polish count, he immigrated from Poland in the 1830s and first joined the watchmaker François Czapek to create Patek Czapek & Co. He was then introduced to Jean Adrien Philippe, a French watchmaker. Patek was interested in this man's keyless watches and asked Philippe to join him when he parted company with Czapek. In 1845 the new company Patek & Co (renamed Patek Philippe & Co in 1851) was born. Their relationship was rather like that of the famous Mr Rolls and Mr Royce – the partnership of a businessman and craftsman. The company produced some of the finest pocket watches ever made and this high quality was also transferred to their wristwatches. Today their automatic movement, with its 22ct gold winding rotor, is the nearest thing to a handmade watch and is extremely sought after. The company also hold records of all their watches, so collectors can easily trace the origins of a watch before they buy it.

Eterna 18ct Gold Automatic Watch, 2003

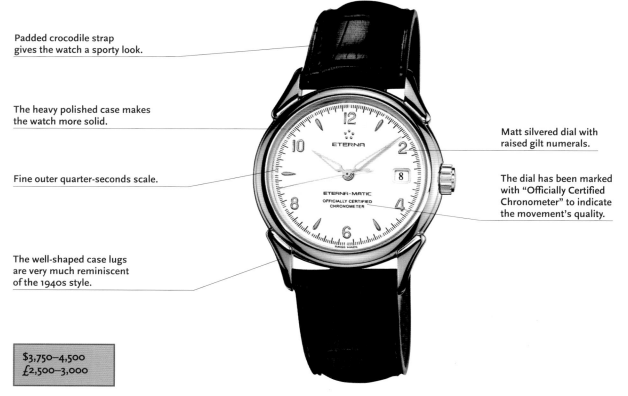

Padded crocodile strap gives the watch a sporty look.

The heavy polished case makes the watch more solid.

Fine outer quarter-seconds scale.

The well-shaped case lugs are very much reminiscent of the 1940s style.

Matt silvered dial with raised gilt numerals.

The dial has been marked with "Officially Certified Chronometer" to indicate the movement's quality.

$3,750–4,500
£2,500–3,000

Patek Philippe 18ct Gold Automatic Watch, 2003

Slim black strap with solid gold fixing screws. The screwheads are visible and give the watch a vintage look.

Matt, white-painted dial with gold half-moon hands give the feel of a 1920s watch.

The gold case, hinged bezel, and case-back make it similar to a pocket-watch case — revealing the company's roots.

$9,000–13,500
£6,000–9,000

The Breguet-style winding button is again very much a pocket-watch feature and is extremely easy to operate as it offers the user a good grip.

▼ The Geneva Seal, created in 1886, is only put on watch movements of the highest quality. To receive the mark a watch has to meet particular criteria to do with the finishing of its movement, such as the screwheads being polished with chamfered slots. The movements must also be finished and assembled in Geneva itself.

Automatic Movements

◀ This view of a Patek Philippe automatic movement shows the large gold rotor oscillator and indicates where it would be positioned on the back of the the movement. The gilt barrel and mainspring are also clearly visible here.

The Geneva shield can also be seen on the smallest plate on the left-hand side. The fine damascening and spot finishing on the nickel plates are there purely to add to the appearance of the movement rather than for any technical reason.

Chronographs I

These two modern chronographs are both very much future collector's pieces and are based on the military style of watches pioneered by the International Watch Company (*see* Military Watches on page 78). This company was founded in 1868 by an American gentleman, Florence Jones, and is based in Schaffhausen on the Swiss/German border on the banks of the Rhine. Jones had a knowledge of the industrialized production of watches using machines, and he set out with the vision of producing low-cost watches for the American market.

The Swiss watch industry very much depended on a skilled workforce but the USA had factories with machines that made watches. Johann Heinrich Moser was an industrial pioneer and he had built a hydrostation on the banks of the Rhine that would use the river to produce low-cost power. There were few takers for this but Jones saw his opportunity and the company moved in.

In 1935 IWC's first airman's wristwatch was created and the aviation connection was born. Such watches incorporated black dials and large luminous Arabic numerals, which became a recognizable general style for the company. The two watches shown here are part of their current range and will no doubt become timeless classics.

The Flieguer chronograph is an automatic model with a screw-on water-resistant case. The watches are similar in look but the Doppel chronograph has an interesting feature in that it has two sweep seconds hands, which enables the wearer to record lap times in, for example, a horse race. This expensive feature makes the piece much more desirable. Large watches such as this have become the vogue, and recent models have been introduced with attractive silver and shiny black dials and Arabic numbers. The Flieguer model was introduced in 1994 and is still made today. It is smaller that the Doppel watch and also has a dressier feel as it is much slimmer.

IWC Flieguer Chronograph, 1994

The brushed-finish case surround has a military look and a soft-iron anti-magnetic core.

Luminous triangle at 12 o'clock.

The subsidiary recording dials give the owner the exact elapsed chronograph time up to 12 hours.

Ultra-clear white Arabic numerals.

The outer minute track has a timing scale down to the quarter second.

Twin round push pieces operate the chronograph.

The day and date windows are not normally found on true military watches.

$3,300–3,750
£2,200–2,500

IWC Doppel Chronograph, 1992

Outer minute scale with one-fifth of a second track for use with the chronograph.

This button is used to stop one of the twin seconds hands, to allow the user to record lap times.

Again day and date windows indicate this is not a true military timepiece.

Large winding crown is screwed down to the case to prevent water getting in.

Ultra-clear white Arabic numerals on a black ground.

Two sweep seconds hands. The hands move off together; the lower is stopped by pushing the button at 10 o'clock.

$7,250—9,000
£5,000—6,000

▶ This close-up shows the action of the split seconds hand. The hand is mounted on top of the single arbor and can be stopped independently to record intermediate times. Such chronographs are 50 per cent more expensive to produce than normal examples. Chronographs also have a special soft-iron inner case that surrounds the movement to protect it from the magnetic fields that are produced near electrical equipment. These fields would cause the movement to become magnetized and therefore upset the timekeeping.

Chronographs II

The development of the sports chronograph began with companies such as Zenith and Universal. They started to produce these watches in the 1920s but it wasn't until the 1940s that large-scale production of them began. At this time the interest in them increased, reflecting the rising speeds of cars and aeroplanes; people who bought chronographs wanted to use them to time events or races.

The watch company Zenith has its roots back in Le Locle, Switzerland. In the 1860s the watchmaker Georges Favre-Jacot was very successful and produced over 1,500 observatory-winning pieces. (There were competitions held within Switzerland in which watch houses would enter special watches to assess how accurate they were. The best were given awards, which were marked on the backs of pocket-watch cases.) Favre-Jacot's company was eventually named Zenith in 1911, when the owner retired. The word means "top achievement" and was chosen to reflect the amount of awards the company had won.

The Zenith model shown here is in a pink-gold case and has an outer scale that, when used with a certain dial, can be employed in production counting in a factory or speed calculating. Zenith is still one of the few watch companies to make its own movements and recently it has relaunched a range of fine watches including a perpetual calendar chronograph; all these new watches are based around its famous movements.

Chronograph watches are very popular today. The round case watches are a lot more common and the vast majority incorporate a simple hand-wound movement. These pieces have just one recording dial for use with a chronograph to record up to 45 minutes. More complicated pieces have three dials to enable recording up to 12 hours. The small size and square case of the Universal watch on the right makes it a particularly interesting piece. It is a more expensive watch to produce than the round-cased Zenith chronograph, and is very much a dress piece.

Zenith Round Gold Chronograph, *c.*1950

Polished bezel – check for damage as they can get dented and become loose.

The fully signed dial with the company star logo is a good feature.

The case lug design gives the watch a robust, conservative look. Case lug wear can often take place and soft solder is used to fill holes – this will detract from the watch's value as it is difficult to remove.

Running seconds hand. You should check that the hands match as they may not be original.

The gold-plated winding button should have the factory star mark on it.

The chronograph operating buttons – if these work the mechanism is operational.

Check the condition of the dial and outer base timing scale as they do get worn and dials like this are expensive to restore.

$1,200–1,800
£800–1,200

Universal Square Chronograph, *c*.1955

Brushed, silvered dial. Check the overall condition as the lacquer on a lot of dials breaks down and pitting starts on the silvering.

The dial is signed by a retailer rather than the maker. This was done quite often but it may make the watch less attractive to collectors.

Black crocodile strap. This would not be the original but this does not detract from the value.

Blued running seconds hand – check that this matches the minute recording hand.

The chronograph operating buttons need to be checked to see if they are working correctly.

Some watches have solid gold buckles on the straps – look for a Swiss assay mark.

$6,000–9,000
£4,000–6,000

• *Zenith chronographs can be bought at reasonable prices and have the bonus of good-quality movements. Universal items are more expensive as they are often quite unusual.*

• *Chronographs have complicated movements that can be very difficult and expensive to repair, due to age. It is a good idea to get a watchmaker to look over a piece before buying it.*

• *Watches in 18ct gold or stainless steel are very desirable if they have good, clean, unrestored dials signed with their factory mark. The watches with chrome-plated cases and stainless-steel backs are less desirable.*

Universal

The watch company Universal was formed in the Jura town of Le Locle. The name was registered in 1898 by Georges Perret and Louis Berthoud. Theirs was a new enterprise that set out to produce complicated watches and chronographs. After World War I the introduction of a new small-size movement suitable for wristwatches enabled the company to make much smaller watches, something it has experimented with ever since.

The company moved to Geneva in the 1930s and went on to produce the first chronograph with a 12-hour chronograph recording dial. In the 1940s and '50s it produced some very interesting pieces with names like the Tri Compax and Aero Compax. The Type Colonial was advertised as being a "water and dust proof watch suitable for the outdoor sports man". In the 1960s Universal also went into the electric watch market using the Bulova tuning-fork movement, which, as the name suggests, uses a very small vibrating tuning fork that hums if placed on a table.

The company, along with many others, suffered when quartz watches were introduced in the 1970s. However, due to the growing interest in reviving old names it was relaunched a few years ago and is still producing quality watches today.

Chronographs III

The 1960s saw an enormous growth in the sales of wristwatch chronographs, largely due to the advances made in chronograph designs toward the end of the previous decade. At the same time automatic watches became both more affordable and, therefore, popular. Naturally, a number of companies started to research the possibility of combining the two developments in a single watch. One of the first was Zenith, who began their project in 1962. By 1965 their Swiss competitors had formed into a coalition that included Breitling, Büren, Dubois-Depraz, and Heuer. However, Zenith had a good relationship with Universal Genève, and that company's expertise in chronograph making was harnessed to the project. Zenith chose to design a new movement from scratch that would incorporate the classical "column-wheel" technique to drive the chronograph functions, as well as a full-size central rotor for the automatic winding. Breitling *et al* adopted a modular approach based on combining separate chronograph and winding elements.

The El Primero has long had a place in the affection of collectors as one of the classic movement designs. This popularity endures for a number of reasons aside from the quality and technical sophistication of the movement. Not least is the story of the movement's development and the fact that the survival of the movement parallels the recent history of mechanical watchmaking. When Zenith turned away from mechanical watches in the 1970s the tools for the El Primero movement were nearly lost forever. Fortuitously no-one at the Zenith manufacture was willing actually to dispose of the tools of the most famous movement. When it was realized in the 1980s that there was, after all, a future for mechanical watches, it was possible quickly to re-establish production. The El Primero is still the model chronograph others aspire to.

Even if there is no particular Breitling that has the resonance of the El Primero, the company has one of the longest continuous histories as a chronograph specialist in the industry. The example shown below is typical of one of its most creative periods.

Breitling Hand-wound Chronograph, late 1960s

Black dial with applied indexes and contrasting subsidiary dials to make them easy to read.

The tritium-coated baton hands and red chronograph seconds hand have all been designed with clarity in mind.

Tonneau case with screw-down case back. There is also a tachometer on the internal bezel.

Flush-fitted glass makes this a robust and durable watch.

$750–900
£500–600

Zenith El Primero, *c.*1977

Two-part, polished and brushed steel case with screw-down case back.

Contrasting dial and sub-dial with applied tritium-coated indexes.

Tritium-coated baton hands and red chronograph seconds hand.

Inner bezel tachometer.

The date aperture is famously between 4 and 5 o'clock on the El Primero.

▼ Zenith's reputation for innovation stretches back to the founding of the company in 1865. However, the El Primero is undoubtedly the star of its history. The movement runs at a still rare 36,000 alternations per hour, compared to the more normal 28,800 p/h. The unitary nature of the movement design means that the El Primero is relatively slim at 6.5mm, even by today's standards.

Glucydur balance and Nivarox balance spring.

Engraved and signed rotor.

The fast-beat movement requires a large barrel spring and is driven by a much heavier than usual balance wheel.

The El Primero's chronograph functions are controlled by a column-wheel sited under the rotor mass here.

$1,800–2,250
£1,200–1,500

Chronographs IV

What sets the Speedmaster apart from other similar chronographs is the sheer history of the watch and the fact that it has been proved in the most testing and critical circumstances. Other watches have also been used in space but none have earned the title "moon watch" quite so convincingly. NASA's long campaign to put man on the moon involved procurement of equipment tested to the most extreme levels possible (*see* page 129). Omega's Speedmaster emerged from the tests as the undoubted winner and went on to prove reliable in circumstances such as the Apollo 13 mission – the space shuttle's return to earth depended on split-second timing. Ever since, there has been a certain mystique to the Speedmaster that other watches simply do not have.

First put into production in 1957, its introduction coincided with the USSR's launch of the Sputnik probe and the beginning of the space age. The brainchild of Omega's star watchmaker, Albert Piguet, the watch stems from the early 1940s, when he was asked to develop a new, ultra-slim chronograph movement. The result was the Cal 321. Just 1in (27mm) in diameter, the 321 was the first chronograph movement to carry a 12-hour totalizer, which allows the stopwatch to record up to 12 hours. At the time it was easily the smallest chronograph movement of its kind. The Speedmaster has been one of Omega's most popular lines ever, and the variety of limited editions are dazzling. The first came in 1969, an edition of 1,014 numbered pieces in 18ct gold inscribed "Omega Speedmaster – Apollo 11 1969 – The First Watch Worn on the Moon" – and the first of these was reserved for President Nixon. Since then the Speedmaster has adopted many guises (*see* pages 128–9).

Movado has always been a strong brand, particularly in the USA, offering a large range including good-quality chronographs such as the one shown below. From 1969 many of their chronographs were simply re-badged Zeniths; the Zenith name could not be used in North America at that time so Zenith bought the Movado brand in order to try to establish a distribution in the USA.

Movado Black Dial Chronograph, 1970

Steel case with slimmer "dress-watch" lugs; this watch was intended more as a dress watch than a chronograph.

The position of the date window at 12 o'clock is unusual, and marks it as a Movado watch.

Slim baton hands.

Leather strap.

The interesting bar hour-markers have an eccentric layout.

$1,200–1,350
£800–900

Stainless Steel Replica of the Omega Speedmaster "Moon Watch", 1990

Black bezel with tachometer graduation.

Sapphire crystal.

Black dial with tritium-coated hour markers.

Tritium-coated baton hands.

Three-part case with pressure-fitted case back.

Stylized heavy lugs.

The bracelet differs from the original watch, pictured below, as is common with replicas.

$1,800–2,475
£1,200–1,650

▼ ► The picture on the right shows Thomas Stafford wearing his Speedmaster on the 1975 Apollo-Soyuz mission. The watches were "flight-qualified for all manned space missions" by NASA on March 1 1965 after an exhaustive round of tests in various extreme environments. Below is the Snoopy Award given to Omega after its watch was used to get Apollo 13 back home successfully.

World Timer Watches

It is no accident that the highest prices achieved at auction for wristwatches have, almost without exception, been for Patek Philippe models. Of these, the watch that reappears consistently at the top of the list is the "Heures Universelles" (World Timer). As is often the case with truly classic designs, the reasons for Patek Philippe's particular popularity with collectors go far beyond matters of finish or raw complexity of the movement. The original HU watches were made in small numbers over a fairly short period of time – obviously a feature appreciated by collectors. These watches have such a following because of the elegant design and the technical solution of a complex problem, which caught the mood of the times.

Prior to World War II few people had any experience of travelling through more than one time zone in a single journey, and time zones themselves were established only 50 years earlier. The growth of aviation as a practical form of transport at the end of the 1930s changed this entirely and inspired the Genevan watchmaker Louis Cottier to work out a solution. His design included a local-time central dial with hour and minute hands, which were linked to a rotating 24-hour ring and bordered either by an independently movable marked bezel or an outer dial ring. Arranged around the central dial the outer rings show time zones and the current hour in each zone. Cleverly, these are linked to the hour wheel so that any change to this through the passage of time or through setting is reflected in the outer 24-hour ring.

Cottier's invention was implemented on both pocket watches and wristwatches by several watch houses including Agassiz, Vacheron Constantin, and Rolex. However, it was Patek Philippe that made the complication its own. Early examples achieve enormous prices at auction – often reaching into millions of dollars.

The Movado shown here, and similar models by Tissot, are more attainable targets for collectors – though quite thin on the ground. The idea still follows the basic principle of a movable time zone ring but does without the rotating 24-hour ring. Instead there is a fixed ring and 24-hour hand – simpler to make but somewhat more difficult to work out.

Movado World Timer, 1940s

Movable bezel attached to outer disc with time zones marked. This is "knurled" to make it easier to grip.

Local-time dial and hands.

Fixed 24-hour ring.

Subsidiary seconds dial.

Extra 24-hour hand.

Gold case and lugs.

Flat single crown.

$3,000–3,750
£2,000–2,500

Patek Philippe World Timer, c.1950

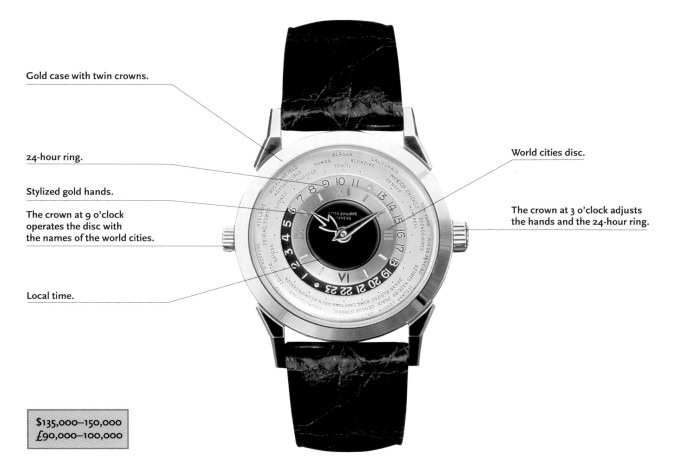

Gold case with twin crowns.

24-hour ring.

Stylized gold hands.

The crown at 9 o'clock operates the disc with the names of the world cities.

Local time.

World cities disc.

The crown at 3 o'clock adjusts the hands and the 24-hour ring.

$135,000–150,000
£90,000–100,000

Modern Patek Philippe World Timers

▶ The latest version of the World Timer offers a further improvement on Cottier's original idea. The button at 10 o'clock allows the local time to be advanced by exact, one-hour increments. That means that the chosen time zone and the 24-hour and city discs move anti-clockwise simultaneously, so that the correct time for each zone is always shown. As Patek Philippe limits production of all its models there is every chance that these new watches will become sought-after by collectors – though not in the same way as the original designs.

Skeleton Watches

The skeleton watch is one of the masterpieces of watchmaking and is built to allow the viewer to see all the watch's workings. It was first produced in the 18th century in the pocket watches of the time. Such examples were very much used to demonstrate the skill of the watchmaker. The movements were pieced out with a floral design but this work had to be done with great skill so the movement's strength was not weakened.

These early watches do come up for sale but are quite rare as the numbers produced were small. The most famous skeleton watch was produced by the renowned French maker Abraham-Louis Breguet. It was started in 1790 and not finished until 1850. Called the Marie Antoinette, it is housed in a gold case with rock crystal covers. This famous company still continues to make watches of this type today.

The first skeletonized wristwatches were produced in the late 1930s by Audemars Piguet but the number of firms producing them has always been limited due to their cost. The example shown on the right was produced by Breguet. It would cost around $150,00 (£100,000) to purchase new because it is made in platinum and the skeletonized movement has a revolving tourbillon escapement. This type of watchmaking is still alive in the famous watch houses, mainly due to the watch collectors and patrons who will pay the price to own a tourbillon watch. The advent of new micro-engineering and machines in recent years has meant that movement plates can be pieced together by machine rather than by hand, although the engraving and finishing is still the job of the master watchmaker.

Skeleton watches are probably the nearest things to handmade watches that are available today. For those that wish to view the movement of their watch but cannot afford a skeleton watch, the classic watch below is a good alternative. An antique of the future, it comes with a crystal back so the owner can admire the work of the watchmaker.

Classic Gold Breguet Watch, *c.*2000

The fine engine-turned silvered dial is a Breguet hallmark and dates back to the early 19th century.

The strap also has a matching gold buckle stamped with the factory mark.

Blued-steel half-moon hands;. they would have been heat treated to produce this colour. The process also stops them from going rusty.

Brushed silver chapter ring against the engine-turned centre.

The hand-stitched strap is fitted to the watch by gold screwed bars.

Gold winding button has the Breguet logo on it.

$9,000–1,200
£6,000–8,000

Calendar aperture positioned at 6 o'clock.

Breguet Platinum Skeleton Tourbillon Watch, *c.*2000

The narrow silvered chapter ring is signed and numbered.

The mainspring barrel cover is pieced and the spring is visible.

The rotating tourbillon carriage is finely finished.

Classic half-moon Breguet hands.

Platinum winding crown has the factory logo.

The escapement is blue in order to give it an attractive appearance.

The hand-stitched strap is held onto the watch by solid platinum screwed bars, and there would also be a matching solid platinum buckle. Make certain these parts are all in place as they are very expensive to buy.

$120,000–150,000
£80,000–100,000

• *The tourbillon, or whirlwind, was invented by Breguet in 1795 to overcome the positional errors in watches. Tourbillons are very expensive to produce.*

• *The interest in tourbillon watches really only started with the first production watch by Audemars Piguet in the 1980s. Before that very few pieces were made. The new watches are able to be produced because of the advance of micro-engineering and the new metals from which the rotating carriages are made. These are, nevertheless, still very expensive so any necessary repairs will be equally costly.*

Breguet

The watch house of Breguet was started by the great master Abraham-Louis Breguet, who was born in Neuchâtel, Switzerland in 1747. He later married the daughter of a wealthy gentleman and this enabled him to set up his own workshops in the watchmaking quarter of Paris. When the French revolution occurred he fled to his home town in Switzerland but returned in 1795. He was a very creative and inventive watchmaker who produced a range of inventions, including a pocket watch winding key that can only be wound in one direction, and a clock that will wind and set your watch at night.

In his lifetime Breguet was called upon to produce watches and clocks for the kings and queens of Europe and his reputation grew steadily. After his death, in 1823, his son continued the company.

The interesting feature with Breguet pieces is that they are numbered and recorded in the company ledgers in Paris, so collectors can discover their watches' histories – the date they were first sold, the cost, and the buyer's name, for example.

The company is based in Switzerland today and, even after 200 years, their engine-turned dials are easily recognizable as Breguets and are also just as collectable as ever.

Military Watches

A convincing argument can be made that wristwatches only caught on in the world in general through their practicality on the battlefields of World War I. Certainly the next world war forced the watch industry to change radically. Military planners on all sides wanted to source large volumes of watches that would be practical to use, economic, and, above all, be able to withstand rigorous conditions. Many of the features we now take for granted were developed at this time.

The influence of these watches on the wider industry is such that there is no concrete definition of what constitutes a military watch – it is only in very rare cases that such watches were not sold onto the civilian market either simultaneously or at a later date.

IWC has an impressive reputation that has been built on many landmarks. Its Mark XI, for example, was the first anti-magnetic military watch, which makes it extremely desirable with collectors today.

Both watches shown here have relatively simple cases with much larger strap lugs than would have been the norm before the war – there is no point in a watch being able to function in difficult conditions if it falls off easily! This feature, combined with the use of centre seconds and a black dial with contrasting markings, is common across the whole sector. The development of this standard can be seen by comparing watches from different times. The Hamilton is typical of the models made at the start of World War II. It is quite decorative, while the Mark XI was introduced in the late 1940s and has a far more functional look.

While the Hamilton watch was standard issue the Mark XI was rarer, which means that the latter is more sought-after today. The Hamilton is a US model and is of most interest to European collectors, where it was never available, while the price of the Mark XI is being pushed up by American collectors eager to own an example of a high-quality British military watch.

Hamilton Military Khaki, 1940

Plain black dial with Arabic numerals and minute track.

The decorative hands are typical of watches made at the start of the war – such hands maximized night-time visibility.

Wide bezel.

Strong, large lugs protect the strap attachments to ensure the watch does not fall off the wearer easily.

Such watches came with either webbed or canvas straps. They rarely survive as long as the watch but can be replaced easily.

A large winding crown was useful for pilots, who would have worn gloves, as the larger size enabled them to grip more easily.

Central seconds hand is far easier to read than the then more usual subsidiary seconds arrangement.

$300–360
£200–240

IWC Mark XI, 1948

Mineral glass pressure-fitted under the bezel.

Large bezel has a matt finish.

The black dial contrasts well with the luminous hands, creating an instantly legible but unobtrusive watch design.

The British government arrow on the dial makes this watch extremely sought-after.

Luminous triangle and quarter bars further aid legibility.

IWC watches were among the first to incorporate central seconds hands on their watches.

Large winding crown made it easier to use the "hacking" device. (When the crown was pulled out one notch it stopped the watch, which enabled the wearer to synchronize their watch with others.)

$2,250–3,000
£1,500–2,000

- *From a collector's point of view the most desirable military watches are those that have a real provenance in the form, for example, of the British government arrow, as is found on the dial of the IWC Mark XI shown above.*

- *Always look for government procurement marks or numbers; nearly all true military watches will have one or the other.*

- *Military watches are sometimes customized to meet government specifications – for example, there are several white dial IWC Mark XIs that were modified by the UK Ministry of Defence. Such items are very rare, and are therefore worth a premium.*

IWC's Anti-magnetic Watches

IWC was one of the first companies to produce anti-magnetic movements and watches. This was in response to the increasing frequency of situations where high magnetic fields were encountered – particularly in military and industrial life. Whereas the earth's magnetic field produces a background of about 80 a/m (ampere meters), large electric engines can develop fields of tens of thousands a/m. By comparison, a non-protected watch will run erratically in fields of a few thousand a/m.

During the 1920s the German state railways requested that IWC develop a watch that was able to resist the strong fields generated by electric train engines. The result was the anti-magnetic Calibre 56 Lépine, which incorporated anti-magnetic materials for the escapement and balance assembly.

The emerging aviation industry was also demanding watches that would be able to remain reliable while being exposed for long periods to magnetic fields. The next development pioneered by IWC was the installation of a soft-iron cage around the movement. This effectively conducted magnetic fields around the movement leaving the escapement free of interference. This neat solution was included in the design of many of the pilots' watches over the years.

Minute-repeater Watches

The idea of a watch being able to strike at the owner's command dates back to the late 17th century, with the pocket watch and the days before electric lighting. During the night the owner of such a pocket watch could hear the time by depressing a button on the case – the watch would simply strike on two gongs or a bell within the case.

These early repeaters employed quarter striking. This means that they struck the hour first and then the number of quarters past the hour. Later minute repeaters do a similar thing but also sound the number of minutes past the quarter.

The wire gongs within the cases are made of a special steel that is a guarded secret among the various watch firms. Known as "singing metal" this is the most important part of such watches as the cleaner the sound produced the easier it is for the owner to hear. The production of the repeating mechanism is carried out by specialized watch makers and the area best known for these is the Joux Valley in Switzerland, which has been the centre of production since the 18th century. Situated across the mountains from Geneva,

the valley is cut off in the winter months by snow and ice. This makes it a very quiet area to work in, particularly suitable for the production of such watches as they require maximum effort and concentration. The very fine mechanisms contain over 300 parts that are hand-finished, and even today companies still produce them in the valley. The workforce has a history of fathers and sons going into this particular watchmaking field.

The Omega watch company was started by brothers Louis-Paul and César Brandt in 1880. They rented an office in Bienne, Switzerland and the growth of the business happened so extraordinarily fast that by 1889 the company, renamed Louis Brandt and Fils, was the largest producer, with 100,000 units. The demand for pocket watches of smaller sizes led to the company producing a small minute-repeating movement along with Audemars Piguet. This was designed for use in a lady's fob or pendant watch. The example shown below still has the look of a fob watch and this may be because the mechanism was simply converted to the more useable wristwatch.

An Early Gold-cased Omega Minute-repeating Watch, *c.*1900

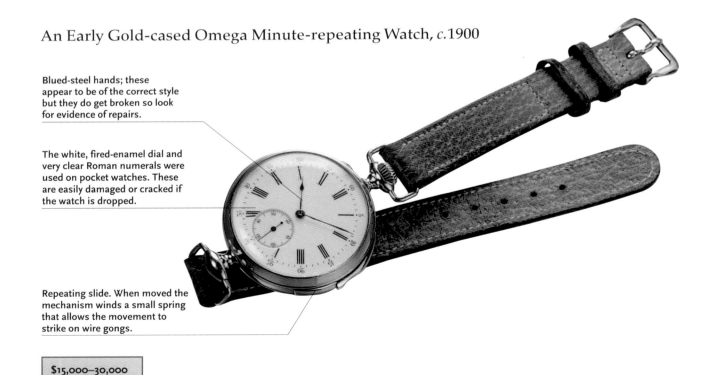

Blued-steel hands; these appear to be of the correct style but they do get broken so look for evidence of repairs.

The white, fired-enamel dial and very clear Roman numerals were used on pocket watches. These are easily damaged or cracked if the watch is dropped.

Repeating slide. When moved the mechanism winds a small spring that allows the movement to strike on wire gongs.

$15,000–30,000
£10,000–20,000

Ulysse Nardin "Genghis Khan" Tourbillon with Westminster Carillon, 2003

Gold moving Jaquemart figures of Genghis Khan warriors on a solid black onyx dial background.

The repeating slide has an "all-or-nothing" piece to stop the watch striking the wrong time if the slide is not fully operated. The Westminster has four gongs and its tone is "Mi-Do-Re-Sol".

The tourbillon revolving escapement, with its gold bridge and polished steel work, is an interesting feature. The carriage revolves once every minute.

▲ A fine view of the tourbillon and chamfered bridge. The black onyx dial plate is thicker than a normal metal dial. The polished wire gongs are visible and you can see how they are shaped around the movement and set at different heights to produce their tones. They must not touch the inside of the case as this would affect the clarity of the sound.

$450,000–600,000
£300,000–400,000

Audemars Piguet Watch, 1923

▶ This superb example of a cushion-shaped minute-repeating watch is in a two-colour gold case. The silvered dial is signed by the famous E. Gübelin, who retailed the watch. The raised gold numerals are classically 1920s in style, as is the whole watch. This styling makes the watch more desirable and wearable. The view of the 29-jewel movement shows the limited space the gongs have to operate within – the hammers are visible at 11–12 o'clock and the moving slide is at the 9 o'clock position (remember this is the back view!). The case back is also signed and numbered; this is always a good sign that a watch has not been re-cased. $60,000–75,000 (£40,000–50,000)

Tourbillon Watches

The tourbillon watch was invented by the great master Abraham-Louis Breguet in 1795 (and patented in 1801). On investigating the reasons for watches giving different timekeeping rates when moved to different positions, he realized that gravity affects timekeeping. So he created a device that makes the escapement and balance turn through 360 degrees continuously, by placing them in a rotating carriage. This created a sequence of positive and negative errors, leading to a natural compensation to counter gravity.

To put the tourbillon into a pocket watch was difficult and expensive so very few were made. The carriage is made of high-grade steel, which has to be heat treated. When this is done there is danger of the piece distorting. The process is still difficult today but there are some alloy metals that can be used. Wrist-watches with tourbillons have been around since the 1940s but they were produced only in small numbers by Omega and Patek Philippe. Today there is a growing number of companies that sell such watches.

Frederique Constant was founded by the Dutch businessman Peter Stas. He decided to create his own watch brand in 1992 with the help of a colleague who later became his wife. The company currently produces around 40,000 watches per year, sold in 36 countries. The watch shown below has an aperture at 12 o'clock in order for the balance wheel to be admired. However, this is just a standard movement with a fixed escapement and not a tourbillon as its appearance suggests. The watch is still an interesting piece for future collectors who wish to see the "heartbeat" of their watch.

The Omega watch is interesting because it is the only automatic tourbillon watch to have a centrally positioned tourbillon on the dial with the hands pointing out from it. Launched in 1948, it was re-made in the 1990s and currently has a nine-month waiting list. The model shown is jewelled with square-cut diamonds. Watches like this have a limited market and a lot of collectors prefer a plain case as the value of tourbillon watches is in the movement itself rather than the decoration.

Frederique Constant "Heart Beat", 2003

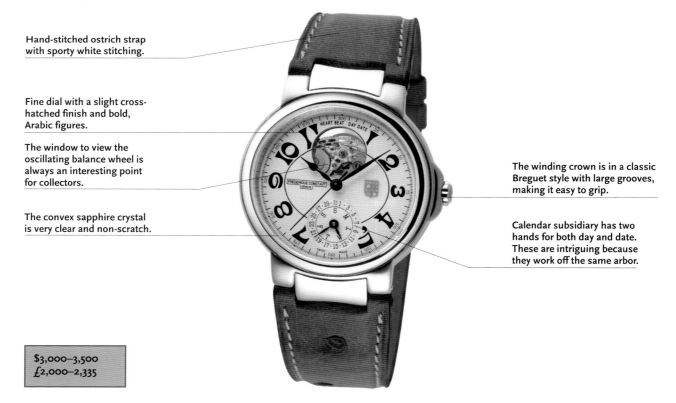

Hand-stitched ostrich strap with sporty white stitching.

Fine dial with a slight cross-hatched finish and bold, Arabic figures.

The window to view the oscillating balance wheel is always an interesting point for collectors.

The convex sapphire crystal is very clear and non-scratch.

The winding crown is in a classic Breguet style with large grooves, making it easy to grip.

Calendar subsidiary has two hands for both day and date. These are intriguing because they work off the same arbor.

$3,000–3,500
£2,000–2,335

Omega Tourbillon Watch, 2000

Hand-stitched crocodile strap with a matching gold buckle.

The styling of the case is based around the 1960s Seamaster watch range, having a heavy design and scalloped-shaped cased lugs.

Channel-set baguette diamonds make this much more expensive to buy new than the model with no stones. (The price below is only a guide as this specific model is a special order.)

The silvered dial has an interesting engine-turned finish and a plain outer minute scale.

$90,000–120,000
£60,000–80,000

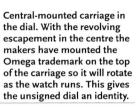

Central-mounted carriage in the dial. With the revolving escapement in the centre the makers have mounted the Omega trademark on the top of the carriage so it will rotate as the watch runs. This gives the unsigned dial an identity.

The winding crown has protective shoulders similar to a sports watch.

Tourbillon mechanism

▼ ▶ These interesting complete and exploded views of the carriage clearly show the escapement and balance wheel. The two red discs are jewels for the escapement. The carriage is highly polished with three arms and screws on the end fixing the carriage together. On the top the pivot on which the whole carriage revolves can be seen. There is also a lower pivot point.

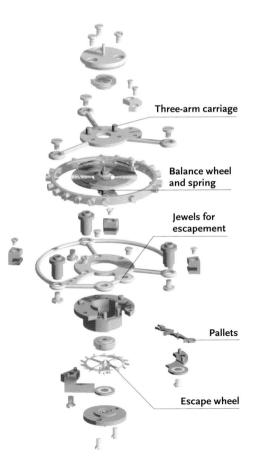

Three-arm carriage

Balance wheel and spring

Jewels for escapement

Pallets

Escape wheel

Reverso Watches

The Reverso watch dates back to 1931 when a French engineer called Rene-Alfred Chauvet patented a design that would protect a watch's glass (in those days the watch glasses were mineral rather than the much stronger sapphire glass used today). His design consisted of a case with a flip-over central section.

The very first reverso watches had "Reverso" marked on the dial and were produced by Jaeger-LeCoultre (*see* opposite). The movements were actually made by Tavannes or Lissca. These early models lacked seconds hands – they came with the introduction of new movements with small seconds hands in 1933 and the sweep hand in 1936.

There have always been a lot of dial variations so there is a great deal of choice for the collector. The cases are made in 9ct and 18ct gold, steel, and gold and steel together. The latter is the most sought after as it goes well with the Art Deco lines and feel of the watch.

Jaeger-LeCoultre acquired the design and patent in 1931, which it vigorously defends to this day, and in the 1930s and 1940s the watch was produced for Cartier, Favre-Leube, and Patek Philippe. In recent years Jaeger-LeCoultre has put quartz movements into some models, but collectors still prefer the quality of a hand-wound watch. The cases have remained almost the same since the 1930s. The three lines on the case, as shown right, temporarily became two in the 1980s.

In the early 1980s Omega came up with the novel idea of fitting two dials, one analogue and the other digital, to the same quartz watch. The purpose of this reverso is to provide a dual look, with one side being a dress watch and the other a full chronograph with alarm. The case-reversing action is very simple as it just pivots at the middle of the case. The watch can even be removed to become a pocket watch! These watches have created a new collecting field. The condition of a watch like this is very important as refinishing such a case may not be possible. The glass also has the name printed on the inside. Such pieces are good buys today but they are not that common.

Omega Equinoxe, *c.*1985

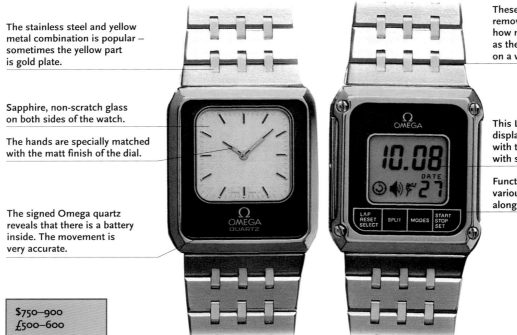

The stainless steel and yellow metal combination is popular – sometimes the yellow part is gold plate.

Sapphire, non-scratch glass on both sides of the watch.

The hands are specially matched with the matt finish of the dial.

The signed Omega quartz reveals that there is a battery inside. The movement is very accurate.

These type of bracelets have removable screw links. Check how many have been removed as they can be difficult to obtain on a watch over 15 years old.

This LCD, or liquid crystal display, has a multi-function use with twin times, a chronograph with split seconds, and an alarm.

Function buttons to operate the various features are displayed along the bottom.

$750–900
£500–600

Jaeger-LeCoultre Classic Reverso, 2000

This example has a stainless steel case but the watch is also made with a two-colour or solid 18ct gold case. The stripes are an important finishing detail of the case.

Two-tone silvered dial with the classic blued-steel hands. These hands have been used on this model since 1931.

Hand-stitched ostrich strap with a matching signed factory buckle.

$3,000–4,500
£2,000–3,000

Fitted with sapphire glass, this watch is well protected against breakage.

▼ With reversos owners can personalize the case with their crest or initials. The one shown fits the watch perfectly, with its Art Deco design and black lacquer surround. Some owners commission fire-enamelled pictures, which are fitted into the watches' case backs.

• Jaeger-LeCoultre produced the reverso during the 1930s and 1940s for a number of other companies.

• The early reverso watches do appear on the market today. These do not have seconds hands and do not have the value of a Jaeger-LeCoultre piece. They are worth about a third of the price of a stainless-steel model.

• The rarest reverso watch was made for Patek Philippe; one sold in a Geneva auction in 2000 for an amazing $186,000 (£124,000).

Jaeger-LeCoultre

This famous watchmaking house has its roots in the remote village of Le Sentier under Antoine LeCoultre, the descendant of Pierre LeCoultre, who was born in 1803. Antoine specialized in instruments and geared mechanisms, but as his enterprise grew he started to produce watch movement blanks and ended up with 125 different types. His sons both joined him in the company and soon began to produce minute repeaters, chronographs, and calendar watch movements, which were then sold to watch companies who would add their name to the finished watch.

Jacques-David, grandson of Antoine, developed a business relationship with a Paris chronometer named Edmond Jaeger. The firm became known as Jaeger-LeCoultre in 1938, but the name LeCoultre was used in the USA until the early 1970s due to a licensing problem.

Jaeger-LeCoultre is now owned by the Richemont group, who have decided to expand the factory and produce movements only for their own watches, rather than supplying other watch houses. Their newest watch has been made for the 200th anniversary of the birth of Antoine LeCoultre. This has an eight-day hand-wound movement and it is sure to be a collector's watch of the future. To buy it new currently starts at $15,825 (£10,550) for a gold case.

Enamel Dial Watches

The use of enamel dial, which involves the fusing of coloured glass over a copper dial, is believed to have started on pocket watches in France and Switzerland in the early 18th century, and on English watches after 1725. These were common up to the 1920s, when owners of small watches often had them turned into wristwatches, and so enamel dials began to appear on these too. However, the appearance of enamel dials only really lasted until the early 1940s. This was due to a number of reasons. Producing the dial was expensive and time consuming so only the top firms such as Patek Philippe could make them. And generally the only colour available was white with dark numerals. In the 1930s customers wanted a more exciting look to their watches so the silvered dial with its two-tone effect became much more popular than the enamel dial.

The major drawback with the enamel dial is that it is prone to getting damaged if the watch is dropped. This causes small hairline cracks to appear, which are at first invisible and only appear when dirt or dust enters the cracks. Sometimes a chip will flake off the dial edge; such damage could not be repaired easily years ago but today can be repaired with a soft, low-bake enamel.

Patek Philippe produced another enamel dial in the 1960s. This watch is highly sought-after today due to the beautiful cream colour of the dial. During the same period a style of colourful dial had become available; called cloisonné, the gold dial had tiny gold wire soldered on it to produce filaments that coloured enamel could then be placed into to make up a picture.

Reviving interest in the lost art of enamel-dial making, Patek Philippe decided to produce a limited edition of 1,000 Calatrava hand-wound mechanical watches (the range had first been produced in 1928). These cost around $12,600 (£8,400) – without an enamel dial the watch would be worth around $11,250 (£7,500). Patek Philippe enamel dial watches seem to draw collectors so this new watch will no doubt be well received at future auctions.

Patek Philippe Automatic Calatrava with Cream-painted Dial, 2003

Raised gold baton numerals, which are riveted to the dial.

Outer minute chapter ring.

Centre seconds hand gives the owner reassurance the watch is still running.

Simple calendar that goes up to 31 days. The date can be changed via a rapid date change on the button.

The case has built-out shoulders to protect the crown – this also gives the watch a sporty look.

$10,500–13,500
£7,000–9,000

Limited-Edition Hand-wound 18ct Gold Patek Philippe Calatrava with Enamel Dial, 2003

Polished case horns that are well shaped to fit the wrist.

The hobnail bezel has been a Patek hallmark design for over 15 years. This involves very skilled production techniques to ensure the design is symmetrical.

Black Roman numerals on a white enamel dial. The earlier watches had very small holes drilled on them so that raised batons could be fitted.

Hand-stitched strap with gold spring bars; these are only used on the very best watches. Here there is a gold matching buckle.

Simple outer minute ring.

Built-out case shoulders protect the crown and give the watch a sporty look.

Small subsidiary seconds dial.

$12,000–15,000
£8,000–10,000

- *Enamel dials are very easy to damage. If a watch's dial has been restored an ultra-violet light will detect this.*

- *Check that the dial is correct for the Patek reference number and that the dial hole is not too big, as the dial may well be a replacement.*

- *Very few Patek watches have enamel dials after the 1940s as the silvered dials had really taken over by then.*

- *Old restored dials yellow with age so look out for this.*

Producing enamel dials

The basic way of producing a watch dial has not really changed in over 300 years. First a piece of copper or silver sheet is cut to the correct size, the dial holes are drilled, and the feet soldered onto it to attach it to the watch (later dials are often fixed via a metal band around the edge).

To add enamel the dial is given a first coat on the back in order to prevent warping. White glass is then ground in a mortar until it becomes a very fine powder. It is sprinkled over the dial plate and fired in an oven at 800°C (1,472°F). Any black specks that occurred during firing are removed with a needle. As the dial may come out uneven it is then stoned flat using water and a fine grinding stone. The process is repeated until the maker is happy with the base colour. Then black numerals are painted on and fired once, at a lower temperature, so the enamel stays intact.

Transparent enamels can also be used to decorate dials. The first example of this is called flinque. The base plate is usually silver or gold, and this is engraved at various depths to produce a shading effect under the transparent enamel. As the light passes over the dial the piece is more or less highlighted. The more common guilloch enamel was popular in the early 20th century and was used in small clock cases and decorative items, rather than watch dials. This was a repetitive mechanical engraving controlled by hand; the pattern was produced by an arrangement of cams, which gave the metal the effect of repeated waves.

Mystery Watches

The definition of a mystery watch is any transparent dial that has no apparent means of moving the hands. This type of watch was first produced in the 19th century using two clear discs working on top of each other. The hands are fixed to the discs and move with them, thus appearing to float. The most famous maker of mystery clocks is the French jewellery company Cartier, which produced some wonderful pieces in precious stones and diamonds, aimed at the very wealthy end of the market.

The Swiss firm Jaeger-LeCoultre had an American counterpart that operated independently. Called LeCoultre, it used the Jaeger-LeCoultre movements but these were just signed LeCoultre. The cases were produced and designed in the USA specifically for the home market, and they were flamboyant in design. In the 1940s the Galaxy (shown right) was produced in 14ct white or yellow gold. This was made in conjunction with Vacheron & Constantin, which was at the time using Jaeger-LeCoultre movements. The watch has diamond batons for the hours and rotating diamonds act as the hands. This watch is unusual because it has two watch company names on it – "LeCoultre" on the dial and "Vacheron & Constantin" engraved around the case back. The model is not that common in Europe but the trade in vintage watches has meant some examples are available. LeCoultre also produced the watch in a simpler gold shell case; at the heart is base metal, with a gold skin fitted over the top. These were made very well and even after 50 years they can look good so always check inside a case for the factory stamp. If it says something like "Keystone" it means it is plated – sometimes it will be marked on the case back with "14ct shell".

Following the lead of such new designs as the mystery watch, various companies tried to capture the lower end of the market. Louvic, for example, created a mystery watch with a stainless-steel-cased or gold-plated watch case, which had paste stones rather than diamonds set around the dial (*see* below). It also used a standard Swiss-made movement. This watch has the appearance of quality but it is just a poor imitation of the fine LeCoultre watch. If you want to create an interesting collection always try to hold out for quality pieces.

Louvic Mystery Watch, 1940s

Bright finished bracelet with large links – this should be checked over for wear.

Floating triangular hour marker with a paste stone.

Bright stainless steel case with unbreakable glass.

The impressive baguette stones are in fact just paste.

Use the winding crown to check that the discs do move in the hand set position.

The centre marker hides the pivot point of the discs.

$150–375
£100–250

LeCoultre and Vacheron & Constantin Galaxy Watch, 1940s

The gold case is signed around the back "Vacheron & Constantin" – the company with which LeCoultre produced the watch.

The baton marks look like they are made up of one stone but in fact there are three stones set together – a baguette diamond would be too costly.

Centre-polished cape hides the pivot point.

Brilliant-cut diamond hour marker in a gold collet setting.

The slim winding crown was designed to be as unobtrusive as possible.

$3,000–6,000
£2,000–4,000

• *The Galaxy was the most expensive mystery watch produced by LeCoultre. The company also made a version in gold shell with no stones.*

• *Various other companies made cheaper copies of this watch – these are interesting but will not create the same collecting interest as the LeCoultre example.*

• *Check the condition of gold shell cases near the lug end as this is where wear takes place and the base metal begins to show through.*

Vacheron & Constantin

This company is one of the oldest watch brands. It was set up in the 18th century by Jean-Marc Vacheron. He gained a good reputation with the French and Italian aristocracy so the company flourished until the French revolution, when clients simply vanished. However, the company struggled on and found a wealthy son of a grain merchant, François Constantin, to back it. He had experience as a watch dealer so the partnership continued to grow.

In 1839 the gifted watchmaker and inventor Georges-Auguste Leschot joined the company and developed machine tools to produce the precision movement more cheaply. One development was the Maltese cross, a component within the spring barrel that ensures only the most even part of the spring power is used, to gain better timekeeping. It was registered in 1880 as their trademark and is still used today.

The company produced some fine repeating watches and chronographs. The movements came from LeCoultre and in 1938 the two companies joined into a close agreement.

In 1980 the company was bought by the Saudi Sheikh Yamani and changed direction, going into the heavily-set diamond watch market. Today Richemont owns the company and it again produces the fine mechanical watches for which it is renowned.

Ladies' Cocktail Watches

The cocktail watch was a product of the high life of the 1920s and 1930s. Such watches were designed to be a way of displaying diamonds – this was made possible only with the development of the small movement's calibre at the time.

Silver generally was used to make watches but the metal discolours and wasn't suitable for cocktail watches as, set with diamonds, it is not easy to clean. However, from the 1950s there were rhodium-plated silver examples, as this stops the discolouration. White gold has been used for cocktail watches as has platinum, which is stronger than gold. A platinum case might be marked inside with "Plat" or "950", which specifies how many particles out of 1,000 are platinum.

The Berco cover watch was produced so that the watch could be transformed into a piece of jewellery. The cover was held down by a small catch at 6 o'clock that, when depressed, caused the cover to flick open.

The other example here is a platinum cocktail watch set with brilliant diamonds. It has been signed by a retailer rather than maker, as is often the case. They are pieces of jewellery and are not at all waterproof as the cases have a simple snap-on back (expensive designs do have a hinged back). The value with these watches is down to the carat weight of the diamonds. Often they look like they are set with large stones but on closer inspection it is obvious they are really a mass of smaller-sized diamonds that have been grouped together. This does make a big difference to the price, but, nevertheless, a diamond-set bracelet is a sign of an expensive watch, so these should all have a decent Swiss-made 17-jewel damascened nickel lever movement. Movements do sometimes get exchanged for more modern mechanisms because the originals are difficult to repair, and they are also not good timekeepers. This has an effect on the value but does not seem to put off buyers.

Berco Paste-set Silver Cover Watch, 1960

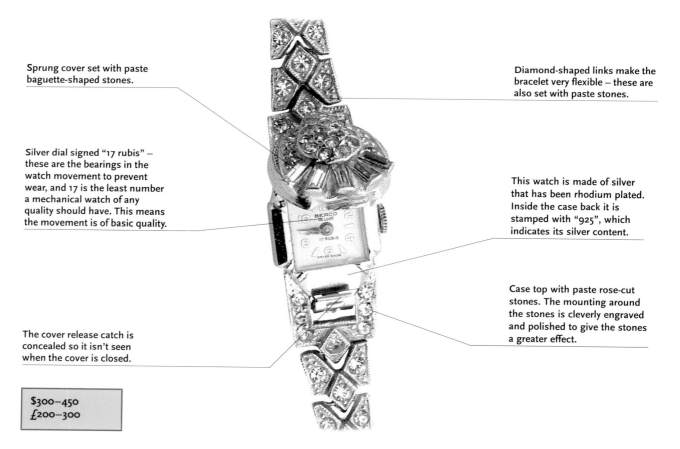

Sprung cover set with paste baguette-shaped stones.

Diamond-shaped links make the bracelet very flexible – these are also set with paste stones.

Silver dial signed "17 rubis" – these are the bearings in the watch movement to prevent wear, and 17 is the least number a mechanical watch of any quality should have. This means the movement is of basic quality.

This watch is made of silver that has been rhodium plated. Inside the case back it is stamped with "925", which indicates its silver content.

Case top with paste rose-cut stones. The mounting around the stones is cleverly engraved and polished to give the stones a greater effect.

The cover release catch is concealed so it isn't seen when the cover is closed.

$300–450
£200–300

Unsigned Diamond-set Cocktail Watch, *c.*1920

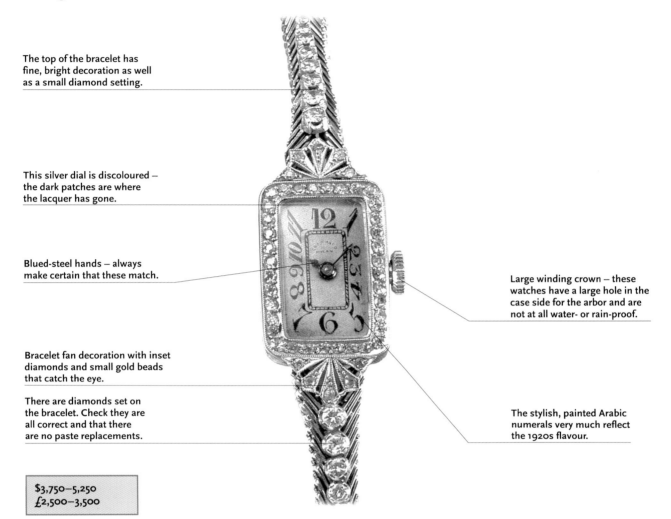

The top of the bracelet has fine, bright decoration as well as a small diamond setting.

This silver dial is discoloured – the dark patches are where the lacquer has gone.

Blued-steel hands – always make certain that these match.

Bracelet fan decoration with inset diamonds and small gold beads that catch the eye.

There are diamonds set on the bracelet. Check they are all correct and that there are no paste replacements.

Large winding crown – these watches have a large hole in the case side for the arbor and are not at all water- or rain-proof.

The stylish, painted Arabic numerals very much reflect the 1920s flavour.

$3,750–5,250
£2,500–3,500

• *Cocktail watches that have names such as Patek Philippe or Rolex on them will be worth 80 per cent more than other examples as they are quite rare.*

• *Be aware that sometimes the movements have been poorly exchanged and are simply glued.*

• *The hinged back case, as opposed to just a snap-on back, is a sign of quality.*

Gilbert Albert

This Geneva-based designer was responsible for some unusual cocktail watch cases. As a young jewellery designer and artist in the 1950s Patek Philippe commissioned him to produce a new style of watch case. The designs he produced were revolutionary and still look stunning today. They were unconventional because he used asymmetric triangles and rhombic forms, which resulted in extreme designs within such a conservative market. Patek Philippe was therefore taking a bold step, especially as it

mainly produced round and square watches. The Albert watches are highly sought-after by collectors and fetch up to $37,500 (£25,000) for a platinum case asymmetric model. They were mainly produced on leather straps of an odd shape, which allowed the watch to sit square when worn on the wrist.

Albert started his own company in 1962 and has since won numerous awards for his jewellery designs. He is still making unusual pieces today, which will undoubtedly be of interest to future jewellery collectors.

Divers' Watches I

Divers' or sports watches are a large part of the current watch market as people like the idea of watches being able to go down to depths of 10,000+ metres. Divers' watches have a surprisingly long history. In the 1950s the Fifty Fathoms water-resistant watch appeared, which could be worn to a depth of 200m (656ft). In the 1960s the Swiss firm of Tissot produced an unusual watch that had a 24-hour dial divided into day and night with a world time inner bezel for 24 capital cities around the world. These watches became popular as the demand for air travel increased. They were also waterproof, although more for swimming-pool depths than for deep sea diving.

In the subsequent decades various technical developments helped to produce watches that were able to reach greater depths with divers. These included the use of synthetic rubber case seals that do not age, rather than the soft metal that had been used, better screw-down winding crowns, and strong sapphire glass. In recent years the space age metal titanium has become used more widely in watchmaking. The metal is very light and stronger than steel and has the same non-allergy factor as gold. The metal is very hard to work with so the links on the bracelets are formed rather than machined. Grey in colour and warm to touch the metal is ideal for watch cases.

IWC produced a diving watch called "The Deep One", which is an interesting watch as it has a built-in depth meter. The watch was discontinued due problems with this depth meter, but the piece has become very collectable as a result. The company now uses titanium a great deal and in 1998 produced a range of watches called GST, which stands for gold, steel and titanium. From this range the "Aquatimer" has a heavy sapphire crystal for working at great depths (*see* pages 96–97). The movable surround is marked up to 15 minutes, which is the normal time spent underwater. As a safety feature, the ratchet only turns one way so the user will never mistakenly be able to add extra time.

Tissot World Time Divers' Watch, 1960

The sharkskin strap is more for looks than anything else as it is not waterproof.

Solid stainless steel two-piece case with a screw-on back.

Heavy plastic unbreakable glass.

The day/night dial is a 24-hour type. This means that the hand rotates once in 24 hours rather than twice. To read it, you must look at what the hands are pointing to.

A movable world time dial, which you can move forward or back by the number of hours ahead (or behind) the place you are in is, in relation to the original time on the watch.

Button for winding and setting the hands.

Button to move the world time bezel.

$1,200–1,800
£800–1,200

Titanium IWC GST Aquatimer, 2003

Rotating bezel, which has an oxidized finish and only moves one way for safety reasons.

Matt black dial with luminous baton.

Heavy sapphire non-scratch glass.

Titanium bracelet. The watch also comes with a fabric strap for divers to use.

Milled edge creates a secure grip for turning the bezel.

Screw-down winding button acts like a submarine hatch.

$3,000–4,500
£2,000–3,000

- *The best deep-sea diving watches have helium escape valves fitted to their cases.*

- *Bezels should have a ratchet so that they only turn in one direction and cases should have screw-down backs and winding crowns in order to stop water entering the case.*

- *Watches over ten years old are not suitable to swim with as the cases may have deformed. These are also generally not waterproof.*

The Ultimate Diving Watch

Currently the Bell & Ross Hydromax is known to be the best diving watch in production. Bell & Ross is a relatively new company – it was set up around ten years ago, originally in conjunction with the German military watch-producer Sinn but it is now independent. The Hydromax watch has a Swiss-made quartz movement with a seven-year cell life. The case has been designed to absorb pressure by having liquid silicon within it. This can be seen only if the watch develops a bubble on the dial as the hands move around within it – the incompressible liquid guarantees absolute water resistance.

Of course a diver could not survive the pressure at 11,000m (33,000ft), or anywhere near that depth, as the pressure would crush the human body, but the fact that this watch can is a real feat of engineering and is a record that may not ever be bettered. This watch is available for sale at around $2,250 (£1,500) and it will definitely be of interest to future collectors.

In 1953 Rolex produced a special watch that was fitted to a submarine but this was not a piece that went into production because it was in a massive oyster-style case with a very large glass crystal. In 1960 it was taken down to a depth of 10,916m (32,748ft). This watch is extremely rare – Rolex kept five examples for its museum and two are owned by collectors. The last one sold for an amazing $105,000 (£70,000) a few years ago.

Divers' Watches II

Since 1983 Ulysse Nardin have been producing divers' watches with a modern look for the younger market. This type of watch heralds a complete change of direction for the famous company. It dates back to Leonard-Frederic Nardin, who set up in the town of Le Locle in 1846. He went on to produce award-winning watches at the 1862 exhibition in London. On the strength of his work he was honoured by representing Switzerland in the 1893 Chicago world exhibition. He is most known for his marine chronometers, which are best described as small clocks with brass gimballed cylinders that keep the movements level as a ship rolls around at sea.

In the 20th century the company received orders for marine chronometers and deck watches (precision marine watches) from the American and Russian navies. These became a major part of the company's output. In 1912 the first wristwatches came out of the factory; these small chronograph watches became its mainstay for many years. The company also produced some very collectable calendar and split-second chronograph pieces but as the demand for mechanical chronometers declined it went into the quartz market.

The man responsible for the rejuvenation of the company's dwindling fortunes is Rolf W. Schnyder who, in 1983, headed a group of investors who decided to bring out new products. One of the most interesting is the "Astrolabium Galileo Galilei", a wristwatch containing an astrolabium. The current watch range includes the divers' watch with perpetual calendar shown on the right. Produced in a special edition of 500, it is unusual because it is both a perpetual calendar and a divers' watch – water resistant to 200m (600ft).

The standard diving watch below has a single calendar window for its simple movement, while the perpetual calendar watch has four aperture boxes, controlled by a complicated movement. These watches are therefore two calendar movement examples at opposite ends of the spectrum.

Ulysse Nardin Marine Divers' Watch, 2003

Unusual black dial with luminous batons and dimples.

Calendar aperture positioned within the calendar subsidiary.

Engraved ratchet time elapse bezel. This only moves in one direction as a safety measure.

The rubber strap has steel or titanium links, on which the maker's signature is placed.

Power reserve indicator, which shows how much power the mainspring of the watch has – this was a common feature of the marine chronometers the company used to make.

Wide-pieced hands with luminous ends for easy recognition.

Subsidiary running seconds hand confirms the watch is still running.

$3,750–5,250
£2,500–3,500

Ulysse Nardin Marine Divers' Perpetual Calendar Watch, 2003

The beautiful blue-lacquer dial was produced in Italy – it has been designed to look like a slice of the deep ocean.

Running seconds subsidiary dial also contains the day of the week.

Year indicator aperture.

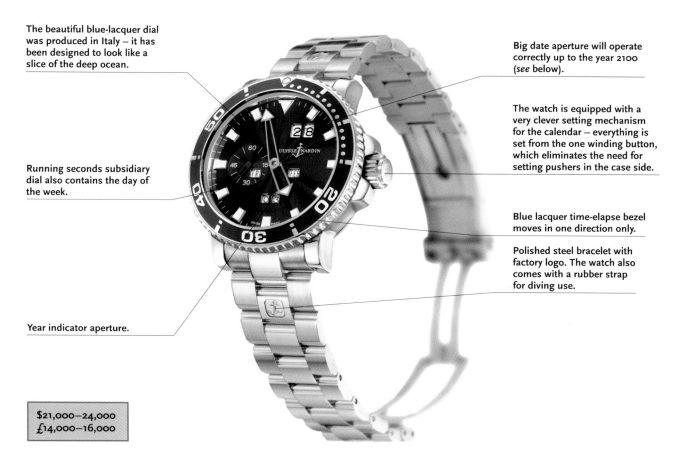

Big date aperture will operate correctly up to the year 2100 (*see* below).

The watch is equipped with a very clever setting mechanism for the calendar – everything is set from the one winding button, which eliminates the need for setting pushers in the case side.

Blue lacquer time-elapse bezel moves in one direction only.

Polished steel bracelet with factory logo. The watch also comes with a rubber strap for diving use.

$21,000–24,000
£14,000–16,000

• *The perpetual calendar watch is probably unique as it is both a diver's watch and a perpetual calendar.*

• *The lacquer dial is an expensive addition that gives this watch a special look.*

• *The single button setting of the calendar is the company's own very ingenious design, created to eliminate the need for pushers on the case side (as these would make it difficult to ensure the watch was completely waterproof).*

Perpetual Calendar Mechanism

The reason for this special mechanism dates back to the year 1582. This is when the Gregorian calendar was introduced by Pope Gregory the XIII to equal out the old Julian calendar, which had 365½ days. To bring the calendar in closer alignment with the tropical calendar the pope advised removing some of the leap years. As a result now one in four years is a leap year – this means there are three years with 365 days and then one year with 366 days.

The first perpetual calendar appeared in clocks in about 1695 and the first watch is thought to have been produced by English watchmaker Thomas Mudge in about 1764.

The perpetual calendar watch has a complicated mechanism of over 100 parts. There are polished steel levers and cams that have notches in them for the months and days; a four-year cycle wheel moves around the mechanism.

Ulysse Nardin has made a unique perpetual calendar watch that allows the dates to be moved forward or back if a mistake has been made in setting.

On 28 February 2100, which is not a leap year, almost all the perpetual calendar watches ever made will need to go back to their makers to either be adjusted manually or have a new part installed for them to display the correct date.

Divers' Watches III

The trend for diving watches has continued to the present day, along with a general trend for a sports look that reflects changing lifestyles. However, it was the success of earlier models that has kept these watches popular. In the late 1960s, for example, a model called the "KonTiki" was named after a famous trip by the Norwegian anthropologist and explorer Thor Heyerdahl, who set out to see if it was possible to reach Easter Island by boat. All the crew wore Eterna watches and these all survived the journey. Thus a new line of sports watches was created and the publicity the company received due to the trip promoted its new watch very well. The current watch of this range (shown below) is a special limited edition. Just 250 pieces are produced each year to mark the trip. The watch uses an inner rotating time-elapse bezel that is protected by the sapphire crystal. The wearer has to push down and turn the bezel to unlock the ratchet and it will then relock once it is moved around. The automatic movement also uses Eterna's famous patent –

the micro balls centre rotor – to wind the chronometer movement. Used instead of normal bearings, which wear out, these ballbearings are made of tough steel.

In 1967 Rolex launched the Sea Dweller. This was in fact created for the oil exploration industry, as its divers had to work at great depths in the hunt for the black gold. In the 1960s divers used conventional compressed gases when they were required to work at greater depths. However, these gases were not suitable for diving watches. The divers spent many hours in a decompression chamber and the fine gas molecules of the helium entered the watch case through the glass and the case seals, building up pressure within the watch. When the watch was brought to the surface of the water again, the gas tried to escape quickly – the only way out was through the glass so this shattered. This was obviously a major problem but during the 1960s Rolex devised a helium escape valve to enable the trapped gas to be released, and this was patented in 1967. The valve was used on the Sea Dweller.

Eterna KonTiki, 2003

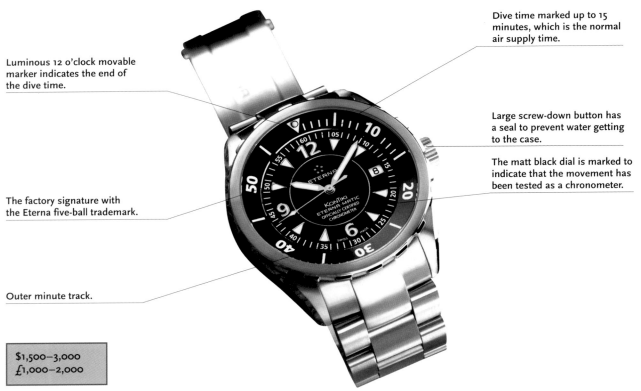

Dive time marked up to 15 minutes, which is the normal air supply time.

Luminous 12 o'clock movable marker indicates the end of the dive time.

Large screw-down button has a seal to prevent water getting to the case.

The matt black dial is marked to indicate that the movement has been tested as a chronometer.

The factory signature with the Eterna five-ball trademark.

Outer minute track.

$1,500–3,000
£1,000–2,000

Rolex Sea Dweller, 2003

Ratcheted time elapse bezel moves in one direction only.

Outer minute track.

Matt black dial with large luminous tritium hour dots.

The triple lock waterproof crown is the best design around because it has three seals to prevent watch getting to the case.

Substantial case shoulders make this one of the strongest cases available.

The hands employ a similar design to that used by the Mercedes car company and are referred to as "Mercedes" by collectors.

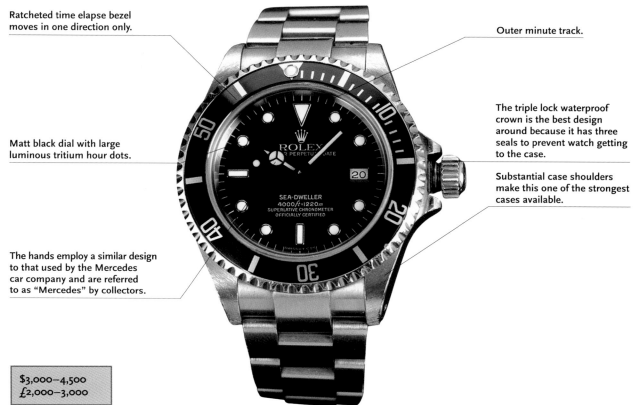

$3,000–4,500
£2,000–3,000

• *This type of watch has a built-in extension link in the bracelet so that it can be worn over a wet suit.*

• *Such watches must have their waterproof seals changed once a year as the seal deteriorates with age.*

• *The winding button must be screwed down before diving with the watch.*

• *Tritium is used as the luminous compound, which is a low radioactive material. There will be a small T on the dial at 6'clock to indicate this.*

The Comex Divers' Watches

One of the most collectable watches is the model Rolex produced for the French diving company Comex (Compagnie Maritime d' Expertise), which contracted out teams of divers around the world to the oil and gas industries.

Rolex actually produced the first watches with the helium escape valve in 1967 just for Comex – it was not until later that year the watches were made available to the public. They are waterproof to a depth of 610m (2,000ft). In the later model the depth was increased to 1,220m (4,000ft).

The Rolex Submariner was the original watch used to fit the new valve – watches already used by Comex. This watch developed into the Sea Dweller and was renamed thus in 1967, although the original Submariner is still produced.

The Sea Dweller Comex watches are clearly identifiable as their dials have a large Comex white logo above the word Submariner and there is also a unique Comex number engraved across the back. These watches were produced in a number of batches that used various models of watch.

The Comex diving company continued its association with Rolex until the 1990s, when it merged into another company.

Digital Watches I

The digital watch is not new but, surprisingly, dates back almost 200 years. Some pocket watches used this form of dial, and were produced by a number of makers, but they were very much a novelty of their time.

The design fell out of use until the International Watch Company decided to gain an edge on the pocket watch market by utilizing a patent from a Mr Pallweber in 1885. The resulting watches were made in nickel, silver, and even gold. Under the dial, instead of a simple gear for the hands there is a complicated mechanism that ensures the hours change at 59 minutes past the hour. Unfortunately these watches never achieved the demand of an analogue dial with hands and are quite rare today. The design was taken up by other manufacturers but the IWC example is the most sought-after by watch collectors because it combines movement quality with the digital dial.

The first digital wristwatches seemed to have been made in the 1930s by a number of companies. There are many around that were made by lesser-known companies such as Awoner Watch Co in Switzerland (*see* below). These watches would have been made for the general market and were sold in chrome-plated, silver, and gold cases.

The company Movado, which is still active in the watch market today, is a name collectors will recognize. It has always had a good name and its watches are of interest as they often seem to have been pushing the boundaries. So it is no surprise that in 1930 they produced a digital-style watch with a silver or gold case. The movement was a 15 jewel with four timing adjustments, so it was made for the upper end of the watch market. This is of interest to collectors, although analogue dials are still probably of more commercial interest.

Awoner Watch Co, *c.*1930

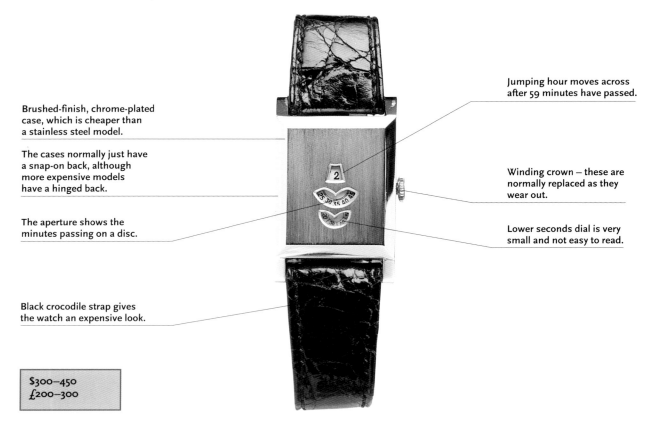

Jumping hour moves across after 59 minutes have passed.

Brushed-finish, chrome-plated case, which is cheaper than a stainless steel model.

The cases normally just have a snap-on back, although more expensive models have a hinged back.

The aperture shows the minutes passing on a disc.

Winding crown – these are normally replaced as they wear out.

Lower seconds dial is very small and not easy to read.

Black crocodile strap gives the watch an expensive look.

$300–450
£200–300

Movado Gold Digital Watch, 1930s

Hour aperture jumps across after 59 minutes.

Minute track, which is marked on a silvered disc. Check the condition of this as it would be expensive to restore.

The case on this watch has a hinged back so the movement simply swings out when it needs to be removed – this feature is a sign of quality.

The pigskin strap with the stitched edge gives the watch a sporty look.

$1,500–2,250
£1,000–1,500

IWC Pallweber

▶ This unusual watch was originally designed by Mr Pallweber and employed a new design of mechanism with his patented jump-hour feature. This complex mechanism has a small device to hold the hour disc at the right hour until the very last seconds of the last minute. When it is released, it jumps to show the new hour.

Digital Watches II

With the development in the late 1960s of the light-emitting diode, or LED, the end was in sight for the mechanical digital watch. One of the first watches produced with this new technology was made by Hamilton. It was called the Pulsar and was the first watch not to have any moving parts. Being a new invention, the watch had a large premium placed upon it and cost something around $1,500 (£1,000), but as the price of the electronic chips fell so did watch prices. Hamilton produced the Pulsar for the top end of the market in a solid gold case, but more common is the brushed-finish stainless steel case and, later, a plated case. The watch made it to the world stage in the 1973 blockbuster James Bond film *Live and Let Die*, in which Mr Bond was seen with it on his wrist, which would have helped sales greatly. The LED movements for such watches consumed a lot of power so the display would remain lit for about 1¼ seconds only. It took two batteries the size of a hearing aid to run them and these lasted around six months. The Far East killed off the American electronic watch industry with their cheaper production costs and the introduction of the liquid crystal display, or LCD.

The Omega watch company have had a long history, dating back to the early 1900s, of providing stop watches and other devices for major sporting events, including the Olympic Games. Scoreboards with the athletes' times are an important part of this and the watch shown, right, is based on this idea. This large watch has a very clean dial of the type used on the main timing boards. Stop watches with LCD first appeared in the early 1970s from Longines and Seiko. They used very low power consumption so remained lit all the time. All these different digital watches do have collecting interest but not as large as that for mechanical watches or chronographs. Repairing them might also be a problem as they are now over 20 years old, so before you buy one make sure the watch operates correctly.

Hamilton Pulsar Calculator Watch, 1973

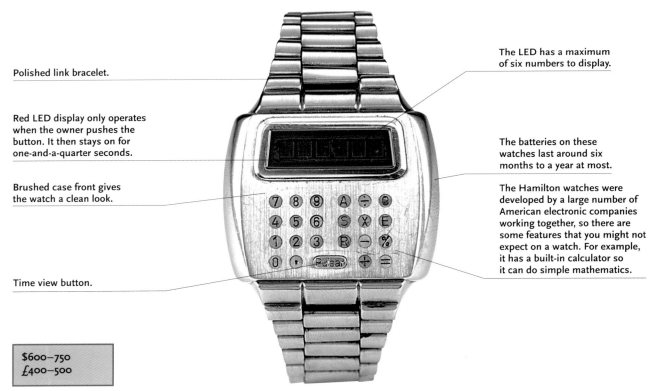

Polished link bracelet.

Red LED display only operates when the owner pushes the button. It then stays on for one-and-a-quarter seconds.

Brushed case front gives the watch a clean look.

Time view button.

The LED has a maximum of six numbers to display.

The batteries on these watches last around six months to a year at most.

The Hamilton watches were developed by a large number of American electronic companies working together, so there are some features that you might not expect on a watch. For example, it has a built-in calculator so it can do simple mathematics.

$600–750
£400–500

Omega Olympic Watch, 1973

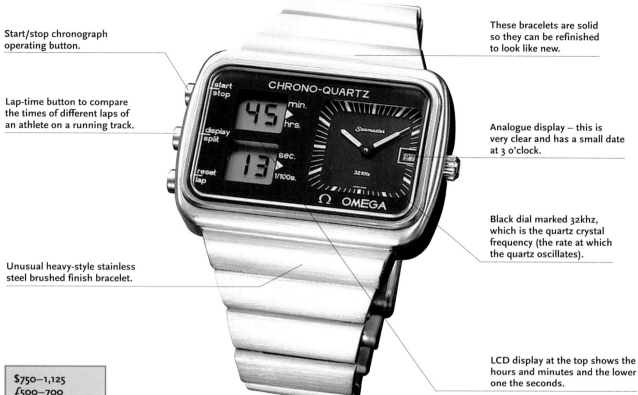

Start/stop chronograph operating button.

Lap-time button to compare the times of different laps of an athlete on a running track.

Unusual heavy-style stainless steel brushed finish bracelet.

$750–1,125
£500–700

These bracelets are solid so they can be refinished to look like new.

Analogue display – this is very clear and has a small date at 3 o'clock.

Black dial marked 32khz, which is the quartz crystal frequency (the rate at which the quartz oscillates).

LCD display at the top shows the hours and minutes and the lower one the seconds.

◄ The dot matrix scoreboard with video replay was invented by the timing division of Omega. This team also produced the 1,000th-of-a-second timing for most events, photo-finish cameras, and the electronics touch pad for swimming events – the latter has helped stop the problem of trying to determine swimmers' times in the water.

Digital Watches III

By the mid-1970s the production of watches with LED displays was being taken over by the making of superior LCD watches. The Japanese started to take a larger and larger share of this market. Seiko, like many Japanese companies, was very good at developing new products. The new LCD watches had the major advantage that their displays always remained visible. They were also a lot slimmer in size and, as the power consumed was much lower that in LED watches, smaller batteries could be used. They also came out at affordable prices. The Seiko watch shown here is the first watch the company produced, in 1973. It has a built-in chronograph and a timing function, and was aimed at being a mass-market watch.

The Omega watch company made watches for the high end of the market. The Omega Digital Time Computer was produced in the 1970s. The watch has an interesting way of setting the time – it uses a magnet that is kept in a clasp; the magnet is held against the watch's back so the time can be set. Unfortunately this was not the most convenient way of setting the time.

The Swiss company Heuer, now known as TAG Heuer, was started by Edouard Heuer back in the 1860s. It developed a reputation for sports timing watches and built up a connection with the Formula One Ferrari team. It produced a watch with a split-second chronograph for the team. The function of split timing is to assess the lap times of a driver. The watch was expensive at the time so was not a great success, and it is unusual to find examples today.

There are a lot of young collectors who like the 1970s look and the technology that went with these times so this is a growing collecting area. However, if a watch develops a fault then repairing it could be a big problem as a new module would have to be fitted and these are often now obsolete.

Seiko Watch, 1973

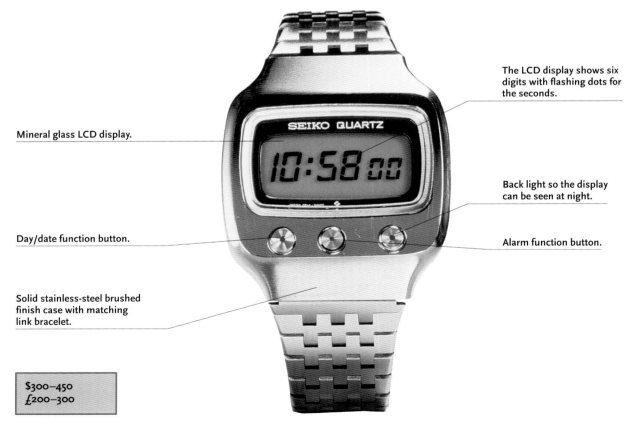

Mineral glass LCD display.

The LCD display shows six digits with flashing dots for the seconds.

Back light so the display can be seen at night.

Day/date function button.

Alarm function button.

Solid stainless-steel brushed finish case with matching link bracelet.

$300–450
£200–300

Omega Digital Time Computer, 1973

Massive brushed-finish gold-plated stainless steel case.

Ruby-coloured mineral glass with the digital display showing hours, minutes, and seconds.

Time view button — the display stays on for only one-and-a-quarter seconds in order to conserve battery power.

The watch case has an expensive screw-on back.

These bracelets have a soft brushed finish and the magnet is held within the clasp for time setting.

$300–450
£200–300

Heuer Split-Second Digital Chronograph, 1979

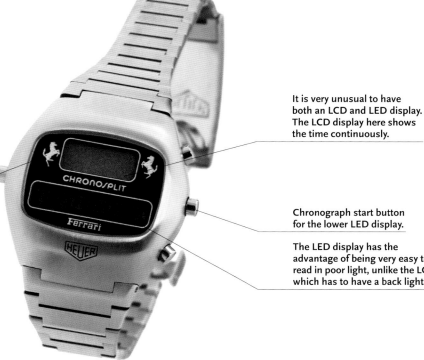

The Ferrari prancing horse logo has been used by other companies over the years, including Longines and, recently, Girard-Perregaux. Watch companies hope to gain new customers with such an association.

It is very unusual to have both an LCD and LED display. The LCD display here shows the time continuously.

Chronograph start button for the lower LED display.

The LED display has the advantage of being very easy to read in poor light, unlike the LCD, which has to have a back light.

$750–1,200
£500–800

Electric Watches

lectrical clocks were produced as early as the 1900s. These early electrical clocks were powered by an impulse sent to a pendulum or moving balance wheel, but there was a problem with the contacts – when they oxidized there was a danger that the clocks would stop. With this problem in mind, in 1952 Elgin and Lip of France announced that it was going to start a development programme for electro-mechanical watches. These were made possible with the development of smaller batteries. The watches used a conventional style balance wheel that had very small wire coils attached. On the early models they used a switching device to excite the balance.

The American watch company Hamilton was one of the first companies to produce these watches, and it did so from 1957. They often came in unusual case shapes, which summed up the new development in watch movement design. Using gold-shell cases was a cost-effective way of making these electric watches reach the mass market. Gold is always the most desirable colour for watches and these have a base metal core with a heavy outer shell of 14ct gold, which means they wear very well. Hamilton also offered a watch with small diamonds mounted on the dial (*see* below). The case shape of this design would not look out of place in the conservative market, but the other examples are very different as they have triangular-shaped cases.

In recent years a reproduction dress model with a chronograph has been produced (*see* right), but this has a modern quartz movement rather than the impulse balance movement. All these watches were produced for the home market and were not widely exported to Europe, so English collectors get very excited when an example comes up for sale. As with all early electric watches it is best to buy a working example as the repairs can be expensive, and sometimes impossible.

Hamilton Van Horn, 1957

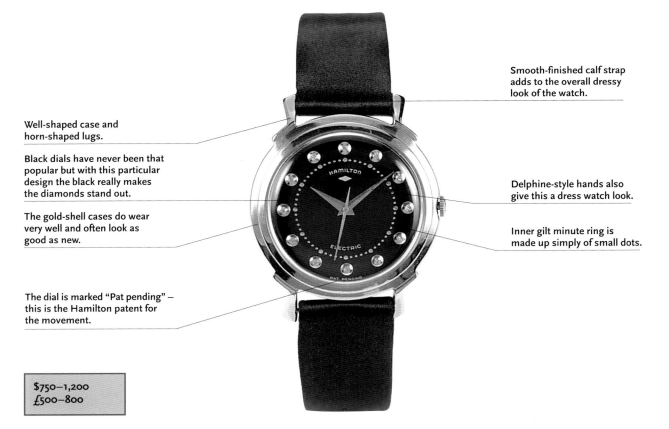

Well-shaped case and horn-shaped lugs.

Black dials have never been that popular but with this particular design the black really makes the diamonds stand out.

The gold-shell cases do wear very well and often look as good as new.

The dial is marked "Pat pending" – this is the Hamilton patent for the movement.

Smooth-finished calf strap adds to the overall dressy look of the watch.

Delphine-style hands also give this a dress watch look.

Inner gilt minute ring is made up simply of small dots.

$750–1,200
£500–800

Hamilton Ventura, 1957

Stepped case waves gave the watch a totally different look to any other watches that were around at the time.

The watch strap has two different colours – gold and black leather.

The dial has a lightning bolt across the dial centre to advertise Hamilton's use of the new electric technology.

The delphine-style hand was usually used on dress watches.

These watches often had a battery cover to aid cell change. Here it was like a coin slot, so the owner could change it easily.

The batons are different again and look like they have just burst onto the dial, almost as though the lightning has just struck.

$2,250–3,750
£1,500–2,500

Men in Black

▶ This style of watch was worn in the recent blockbuster *Men in Black*. It is odd to think that the watch was produced over 40 years ago, but even today examples still look far ahead of their time. The left-hand watch is the 2002 example, known as MKII MIDII, while the right-hand one is a much older example. The modern pieces, unlike the originals, can be fitted with a chronograph movement, but they have a quartz, not an impulse balance, movement. These future collectables at the moment sell for around $645 (£430).

Motorist Watches

The gentleman motoring enthusiast was catered for even in the early days with pocket watches engraved with motoring scenes. The well-known firm Dunhill opened for business in London in 1893. Their exclusive pieces included special waterproof clocks for the open cockpit and pocket chronograph watches, although they did not go as far as producing a radiator watch. This was first done by a young watchmaker and engineer named Georges Schaern, who started a new watch company in Switzerland in 1918 that he called Mido. The 1920s was an exciting time for the motoring gentleman and one of the most sought-after cars was the Bugatti, which had a classic trade-marked horseshoe-shaped radiator with an oval red enamel plaque. Schaern saw a business opportunity when he looked at the shape of the Bugatti radiators. He felt that a watch case that was designed to mirror this shape would work well as owners were so proud of their cars that they would no doubt like to be reminded of them at all times. So he set about designing a miniature Bugatti to be worn on the wrist! Schaern built up a collection using other car radiators, including Chevrolet and Fiat, and developed a relationship with the motoring associations to encourage client loyalty. This was a good way of moving up in society and even the King of Spain became one of his clients. The most desirable example today would be the Bugatti, due to the fact that the cars themselves are very expensive and owners like the history that comes with such pieces. It's believed that Mido only produced around 20 examples of this model so they are also the rarest models around.

The latest Bugatti watch is being produced by Parmigiani, which is a relatively new company. Started ten years ago, it has gained its reputation in the restoration of fine antique watches. This latest watch, a marvel of design, follows the new car that is soon to be released (*see* box, right). This piece will certainly be a collector's item of the future due to its novel design.

Mido Chevrolet Radiator Grill Watch, 1920s

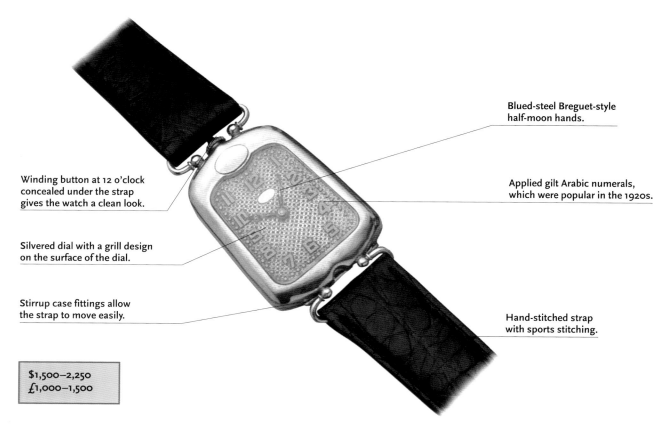

Winding button at 12 o'clock concealed under the strap gives the watch a clean look.

Silvered dial with a grill design on the surface of the dial.

Stirrup case fittings allow the strap to move easily.

Blued-steel Breguet-style half-moon hands.

Applied gilt Arabic numerals, which were popular in the 1920s.

Hand-stitched strap with sports stitching.

$1,500–2,250
£1,000–1,500

Mido Bugatti Radiator Watch, *c.*1920

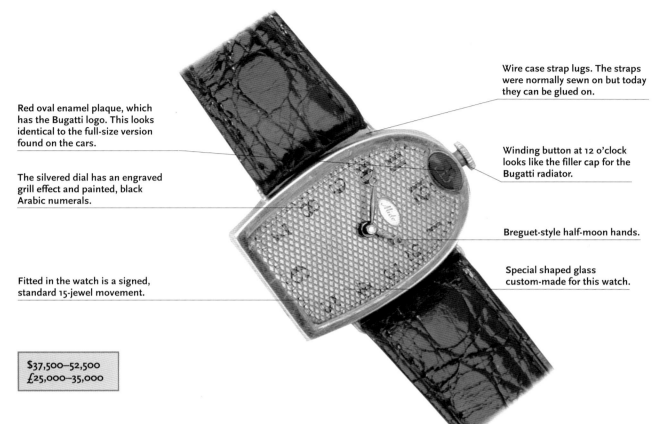

Red oval enamel plaque, which has the Bugatti logo. This looks identical to the full-size version found on the cars.

The silvered dial has an engraved grill effect and painted, black Arabic numerals.

Fitted in the watch is a signed, standard 15-jewel movement.

Wire case strap lugs. The straps were normally sewn on but today they can be glued on.

Winding button at 12 o'clock looks like the filler cap for the Bugatti radiator.

Breguet-style half-moon hands.

Special shaped glass custom-made for this watch.

$37,500–52,500
£25,000–35,000

Parmigiani Watch

◄ This unique watch was created in 2002 as a driver's watch, to go with the new Bugatti Veron car. This car is judged to be the fastest car in the world, with 1001 horse-power. The 18ct white-gold watch has a movement that is unusual because it has five plates and the wheels are visible in-between, to reflect a gear box design. The watch has a ten-day power reserve and is wound up using a special spring-driven winding pen. The watches will be offered to the new car buyers. Priced at around $180,000 (£120,000) they are significantly cheaper than the cars, which cost $750,000 (£500,000).

Coin Watches

Corum was founded in 1924 by Gaston Ries and has recently been taken over by the super-creative Severin Wundermann. The company has always cultivated the niches of watchmaking, whether it be haute horlogerie pieces or coin watches. It was not the first to notice the challenge and possibilities such gold coins represented, but nevertheless it made this speciality its property, at least until Royce came along. Apart from its copies of the Corum watches, Royce, which was originally registered by Sylvan Kocher & Cie in 1930, has had little impact on the watch world, and the name Royce seems later to have been used only in relation to the Corum copies rather than the company itself. These copies are known as Swank watches and are not highly sought-after so are usually very inexpensive.

The challenge of incorporating coins into a watch's design meant that some technical mastery had to be employed. Although the $20 "Double Eagle" is a comparatively large coin, it nevertheless leaves only a sliver of space within which to work. With this in mind, the $10 "Eagle" becomes an even more impressive achievement.

To make a coin watch the coin is first cut in two along its edge. One half of the coin forms the dial of the watch, over which crystal is mounted to protect the soft surface of the gold and the vulnerable hands. The second half is milled out to allow the insertion of a necessarily ultra-slim movement, the two halves being held together by a gold band decorated to replicate the milled edges of the coin.

As well as watches made using $10 and $20 gold coins, there are examples made with a variety of other gold coins, including British sovereigns and florins, and Italian lire. The Mexican 50 pesos coin, in particular, has often been used due to its generous dimensions.

Over the years several other watch companies have made coin watches – usually in limited numbers – including Patek Philippe, Vacheron Constantin, Jaeger-LeCoultre, and Paul Buhre. Piaget have also been active in this field for many decades. Producing the movements to fit such restricted volumes gave the company the impetus to establish themselves as one of the leading specialists in ultra-thin movements.

Royce Copy of a Corum Watch, 1975

Dial pressed with coin design.

Domed crystal fixed by a gold band.

$20 dial marked "In God We Trust".

Steel baton hands.

Pressed maker's mark.

Gold lugs.

$150–225
£100–150

Corum $20 Automatic Watch, 1990

Straight lugs.

Two-part heavy case with graduated bezel and milled band.

Genuine $20 coin used for dial. It is marked with "In God We Trust".

Baton blued-steel hands.

Gold crown with diamond cabochon.

The reverse is engraved with the profile of Liberty encircled with a halo of 13 stars.

The engraving on the coin shows a bald-headed eagle carrying an olive branch and arrows in its talons.

$6,750–7,500
£4,500–5,000

Piaget Purse Coin Watch

▶ This purse watch by Piaget is typical of that company's work since the 1920s. A secret catch flips up the face of the coin from within the milled edges to reveal a watch attached to the heart of the coin by a hinge. Usually these watches are only signed on the watch itself, and the interior of the coin. Similar watches by other makers are virtually indistinguishable in terms of design. This is worth $6,750–7,500 (£4,500–5,000).

Watches with Provenance

Collectors are always told to look for and preserve any paperwork that accompanies a watch. The reason for this is simple – paperwork illustrates and proves the watch's history. This gives a prospective buyer an added layer, not just of confidence but interest too. Antiquorum's sale in November 2000 in Geneva featured this silver military chronograph from Omega, right, which, in itself, would have been much prized. However, the watch sold for far above its value as a vintage watch because it was accompanied by a service guarantee made out in the name of T. E. Shaw, otherwise known as Lawrence of Arabia. This provenance ensured a hammer price of Sfr86,000, paid by the Omega Museum.

This should really be no surprise given the enormous value placed on celebrity ephemera – the major auction houses have regular sales devoted to just this area. Just how much premium should be attached to a watch is certainly no science. The Lawrence Omega reportedly went far over its private estimate (Antiquorum was not sure enough to publicize it). Among the factors that can affect the price are the importance of the watch to the owner – an Elton John-owned Franck Muller might attract less of a premium than his status would suggest given the number of watches he has apparently bought.

An unexceptional but attractive Patek Philippe was recently sold at Christie's for nearly double its estimate. Again the reason was the watch's owner, in this case Elizabeth Taylor, identified by the inscription on the back: "W'I'N DY GARU DI" (Welsh for "I love you"). The watch was given to her by Richard Burton on the set of their 1963 film *Cleopatra*.

Another form of provenance that can add value is a special commission by a celebrity. The "Slytech" Mare Nostrum is a reissue of the timepiece designed by Officine Panerai for the Italian Navy in the 1940s that was never produced due to the outbreak of World War II. Keen watch collector Sylvester Stallone knew of the design and asked Panerai to make him a special edition.

Omega Gold Chronograph, *c.*1925

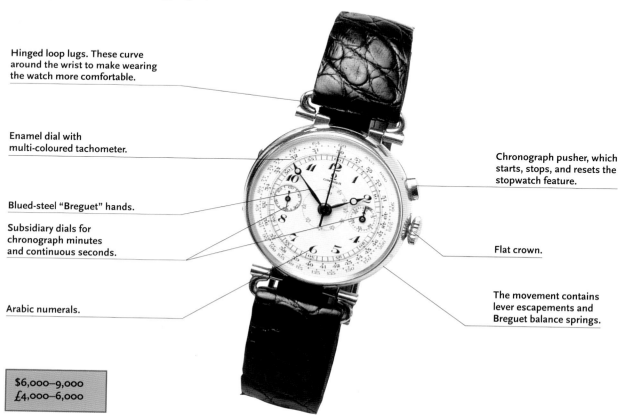

Hinged loop lugs. These curve around the wrist to make wearing the watch more comfortable.

Enamel dial with multi-coloured tachometer.

Blued-steel "Breguet" hands.

Subsidiary dials for chronograph minutes and continuous seconds.

Arabic numerals.

Chronograph pusher, which starts, stops, and resets the stopwatch feature.

Flat crown.

The movement contains lever escapements and Breguet balance springs.

$6,000–9,000
£4,000–6,000

Omega Military Chronograph, 1912

Enamel dial with painted Arabic numerals. There are red 24-hour markers below these.

Subsidiary dials for chronograph (for 15 minutes) and continuous seconds.

Hinged lugs.

Pink-gold chronograph button at 6 o'clock.

Polished silver, three-part case with hinged case-back.

Blued-steel "Breguet" hands.

Large pocket-watch type crown.

$60,000–75,000
£40,000–50,000

• *These two watches are similar in look and date and both are collectable in their own right, but the Lawrence watch, above, is of a much higher value purely because of its provenance (without which the value drops to $4,500–6,000 (£3,000–4,000).*

• *Omega have taken advantage of the value of provenance by producing a limited-edition 007 watch with the 007 logo running across the face.*

• *Watches with enamel dials do suffer from cracks; have a close look as sometimes the cracks can be bleached out to hide them.*

Lawrence of Arabia

T. E. Lawrence was born in 1888 in Tremadoc, Wales. After reading modern history at Oxford, Lawrence joined the British Museum's archaeological expedition to the ancient Hittite city of Carchemish in Turkey. He later travelled to Sinai where he learned Arabic – an experience that made him a natural candidate to join British Military Intelligence in Cairo at the outbreak of World War I in 1914. Lawrence used his contacts and skills to develop relationships with the Arab peoples, in revolt from the rule of the Ottomans.

He played a crucial role in unifying and organizing the disparate forces led by the sons of the Sharif of Mecca, particularly Faisal who was to become King of Iraq. Lawrence participated in the Paris Peace Conference in 1919, but was unsuccessful in his efforts to promote Arab independence in the face of French and colonial India's territorial ambitions over Syria and Mesopotamia. He resigned and enlisted in the Royal Air Force under the name of J. H. Ross in an attempt to escape publicity. In 1923 he joined the fledgling Tank Corps as T. E. Shaw. It was during this period that he wrote *The Seven Pillars of Wisdom*. He rejoined the air force in 1925 and served as an enlisted man until 1935. He died that year following a motorcycle accident in Dorset.

Novelty Watches I

Long before the invention of the Swatch watch, French company Lip commissioned Roger Talon to design a range of watches in a new plastic material. Lip was founded over a 100 years ago by Frenchman Emmanuel Lipman and produced a wide range of pocket watches and then wristwatches. To head off Swiss competition, Lipman decided to enter the precision watch market and had his watches endorsed in 1936 by the National Observatory in Besançon. The company also went on to produce some of the early electric watches with American firm Elgin.

Roger Tallon was born in 1929 and is a well-known designer who started his career in electrical engineering; he went on to become an important industrial designer. Lip also used other designers such as Rudi Meyer and Michel Boyer, who helped it to gain a market share against strong Swiss competition. The company changed hands in 1973 and with the quartz watch market growing there was more competition.

The first Swatch plastic watch was designed in the early 1980s by Jacques Muller, Ernst Thonke, and Elmar Mock. The aim of the design was to build the movement into the case so that the case was not a separate part, as it is in all other watches. Swatches brought a major transformation in the watch market, which had been suffering years of decline with the Asian watch boom. The watch was so successful that by 1992 the 100 millionth watch had been produced. Swatch gained publicity by employing famous artists to create special pieces that had limited production runs – sometimes they were not even sold but given out to special clients and the press.

The boom time for Swatches started with the special Swatch auction in Italy, and, in the early 1990s, Sotheby's and Christie's also started selling them. Who would have thought that fine art auction houses would be selling such pieces, but times changed – those were the days of easy new money in Italy. However, over the years the market has changed again so, although Swatches were once worth more than a gold Patek Philippe example, they have lost out now to the the classic market pieces.

Vivienne Westwood Scuba Swatch, 1990

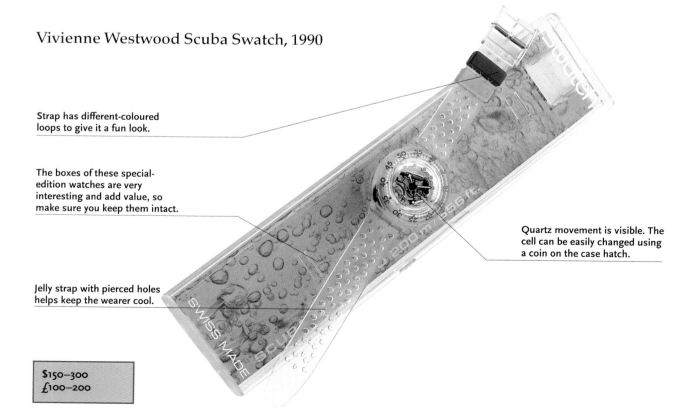

Strap has different-coloured loops to give it a fun look.

The boxes of these special-edition watches are very interesting and add value, so make sure you keep them intact.

Jelly strap with pierced holes helps keep the wearer cool.

Quartz movement is visible. The cell can be easily changed using a coin on the case hatch.

$150–300
£100–200

Tallon Lip Watch, 1974

Black plastic case – these do tend to mark so try to find an unmarked piece.

The strap has a clean attachment to make it look as though it is one piece. Because of this, it would not be easy to replace.

$600–900
£400–600

Smooth red-painted winding crown has been placed at 2 o'clock, which is a very unusual position.

Matt black dial with a very simple orange hour baton and white minute marks gives this watch a 1970s look.

The added slots give the strap a nice design feature.

- *Such novelty watches must be unworn – particularly with special-editions as this is part of their value.*

- *Swatch produced a platinum model a few years ago, and examples do appear at auction and fetch around $750–1,050 (£500–700).*

- *The Olympic Games watches made by Swatch would make an interesting collection. The games are held every four years so there are a number to collect.*

The Rise of the Swatch Watch

The Swiss watch industry was in depression at the end of the 1970s. There had been large job cuts – the workforce of over 100,000 watchmakers was cut by over half due to Far East competition. To try and boost the failing industry the Swatch Watch was created. The Swatch has a one-piece case so when it is made everything goes in through the front, an easy method for machinery. Once the dial, hands, and glass are all installed, and because there is no back to open, there is not a water seal problem, which makes these watches waterproof.

The company later moved into producing traditional automatic movements (*see* page 114). It made quartz movements, then automatic ones, and with new seasons' pieces coming out all the time there is always going to be a new model to buy.

One of the recent range of models has been the James Bond collection, with each new watch being named after one of the films. These are highly collectable due to the films being so successful worldwide, and both Swatch collectors and film collectors will pay a premium to own one.

Novelty Watches II

By the early 1990s Swiss watch firms had seen a major reversal of fortune, with the mechanical watch now being recognized as a quality product, as, for most people, the timekeeping of such watches is accurate enough. The Swatch company, which started with a wide range of quartz pieces, began to sell the traditional automatic movement watches. These new pieces had the same interesting look, with the movements visible, but now came in a metal-clad case called the "Irony". The case was available in stainless steel or aluminium and some were fitted on sprung metal bracelets.

The Tissot watch company is part of the Swatch group, which also includes the major makers Breguet, Omega, and Blancpain. Tissot had a tough time in recent years with overseas competition but the company has had a number of innovative ideas to try to recapture the market. In the early 1970s it produced a most interesting piece called the Idea 2001. This watch was transparent and made of synthetic material, which gave it the appropriate '70s look. The movements were an original Tissot design, with plastic calibres that were self-lubricating when used in conjunction with moving steel arbors. These original 1970s pieces do come up for sale and can be bought at reasonable prices. Try to locate examples that are unworn, as trying to replace old, worn straps would be difficult – if not impossible.

The company also had major success with the Rock watch, whose case was made out of the very hard mineral granite. This came in various colours, from dark grey to a light pinky grey, and because it was solid there was no problem with the colour coming off, as there is with metal cases that have been coated. To launch the watch Tissot did a massive amount of advertising, which helped to give the brand a large boost and put it firmly back in the marketplace. Wood-cased watches followed but were not as popular.

Irony Automatic Swatch, 2001

The metal-clad plastic case was a new idea in case design.

These movements are not built into the case like Swatch's quartz models but are still visible. For example, the watch escapement can be seen operating through the plate.

Brass is the material used for movements on most watches of quality.

Large winding crown helps to make the watch water-resistant.

Twin chapter rings – minutes are shown on the outer ring and 1–59 seconds on the inner one.

$75–150
£50–100

Tissot Idea 2001, 1971

Unbreakable plastic glass is used as it is less expensive than a sapphire crystal.

Silvered inner chapter ring is below the glass so that it does not get marked when the watch is used.

Plastic and metal wheels are used in this movement.

Watching the balance wheel swing is fascinating.

Special smooth leather strap with an inset white detail line down the centre.

TISSOT SYNTHETIC

Synthetic case with a bark finish allows the clear movement to stand out.

Winding crown is water-resistant, as with most watches that are produced today.

IDEA 2001

$150–300
£100–200

- *Swatch have produced many hundreds of models so there is a wide range of affordable pieces for collectors.*

- *The original box and paperwork add considerably to a Swatch's value.*

- *The early plastic Tissot models are interesting to collect, but only worth it if they are in mint condition.*

- *Tissot produced watches with granite cases as well as wooden cases; the market is limited but they could be of interest in the future.*

The Art Swatch Watch

Some very special Swatch pieces were produced in small numbers, such as the Kiki Picasso. This was the first Art Swatch and is still the most desirable model. Only 140 pieces were produced, around 1985. The prices achieved for this model were impressive – in 1993 it was rated at $25,000–40,000 (£17,000–27,000) – this was based on a piece being in mint condition with its original box and paperwork. Limited-edition watches are sometimes available through the Swatch collectors' club and this is also a good source of information. The Italian Swatch market was the largest and it was not until 1992 that Swatch took the English market seriously and launched a limited-edition watch for Christmas in London. The Chandelier watch was presented in a plain wooden box with a molten glass bed to receive the watch, together with a newspaper-style guarantee certificate. On the opening day over 400 people queued up to buy this watch at 10 o'clock and by 3 o'clock 1,000 watches had been sold. The selling price was £45 ($67.50), but within two days the trading price had risen to £200 ($300). The heady days of this sort of increase has finished but the publicity it created for Swatch was beyond the price in getting the brand recognized.

Today the market is much more realistic and the average collector can build up an interesting collection without having to spend a large amount of money, simply by buying examples that appeal to them rather than what current fashion dictates.

Patek Philippe I

The famous company Patek Philippe was first formed in 1839. Since then it has always been known for its quality watches (*see* page 64). In the 1920s the company had serious problems because their American clients were not ordering watches due to a huge economic downturn. It was saved when the brothers Jean and Henry Stern bought it in 1929; they were established dial and spare-part manufacturers.

The 1930s were tough for all the Swiss watch companies due to World War II and the fact that they were part of a landlocked nation, which meant that they were cut off from their client base around the world. The wristwatch had taken over as the main product that clients desired, as pocket watches were becoming less useful; soldiers were wearing wrist-watches, so the end was in sight for the pocket watch.

Patek Philippe decided to produce a range of models aimed at being more commercial. Called Calatrava, the range was named after the ancient Spanish order of knighthood founded in 1158 by the Cistercian abbot in the Spanish town of Calatrava, near Ciudad Real. The main purpose of the order was to fight off the Arab invaders.

The symbol and ornate cross is now a recognized company design and is marked on all its winding buttons. In 1932 the company produced Calatravas in quite a small-size case – this was actually the standard size for most other watches apart from the Rolex Oyster. The look of the watch, with its round dial, is simple and the movement is hand wound. The watches were produced in stainless steel, 18ct yellow gold, pink gold, and, the rarest, platinum. There were different dials, some with unusual raised Arabic numerals, and the enamel dial did make an appearance. Calatravas are still produced today.

Of the two Calatravas shown here both are collectable, but the steel model is much rarer and highly sought-after because of this.

Gold Calatrava, 1940s

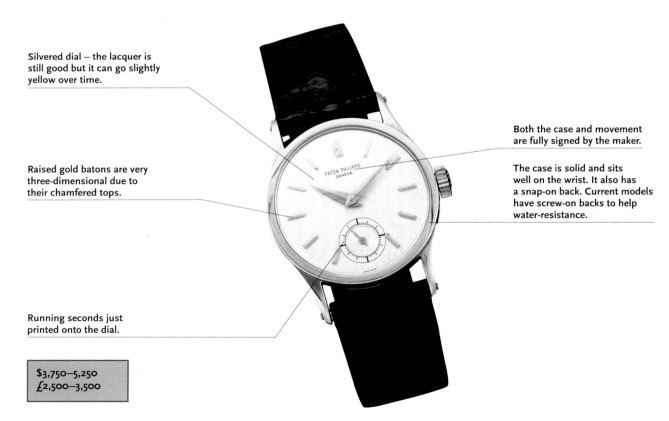

Silvered dial – the lacquer is still good but it can go slightly yellow over time.

Raised gold batons are very three-dimensional due to their chamfered tops.

Running seconds just printed onto the dial.

Both the case and movement are fully signed by the maker.

The case is solid and sits well on the wrist. It also has a snap-on back. Current models have screw-on backs to help water-resistance.

$3,750–5,250
£2,500–3,500

Stainless Steel Calatrava, 1940s

Raised Arabic numerals —
these are quite unusual on
such models but are often
found on the earlier models
while batons are used on
more modern examples.

These figures are cut out
and riveted to the dial via
very small holes.

Printed subsidiary seconds dial.

The dial has a two-tone silvering
effect with a silvery chapter and
matt centre to give a contrast.

The steel cases are more desirable
as white is a popular colour in
today's market and fewer were
produced than the gold models.

The case has a snap-on back
and the Calatrava cross and serial
number of the watch is inside.

The black strap is not sewn
on but has a detachable spring
bar so it is very easy to change
the straps when necessary.

$4,500–6,000
£3,000–4,000

• *The most sought-after model
of the Calatrava range is the
1929 Platinum model with
a triple calendar and moonphase; only about four are
recorded – the last model
sold for over $1.5 million
(£1 million).*

• *As with all its watches,
Patek Philippe has records
of each Calatrava and what
it looked like on the day it
left the factory.*

• *With such expensive watches
you should get a professional
watchmaker to look at an
example's movement before
buying. Such movements can be
expensive to repair and it is not
unknown for damage to have
been done by poor repairers.*

The Patek Philippe Millionaire Collectors

In the early 20th century two unique American collectors became the driving force behind the complicated watch market. These two great collectors were the multi-millionaire automobile manufacturer Charles Packard from Warren, Ohio, and private banker Henry Graves Jr from New York. They never met but had a common interest in watches. Both commissioned Patek Philippe to produce some of the finest and most expensive complicated watches ever produced and this became a golden age for Patek Philippe. The world's most complex watch, with 24 complications, was produced for Henry Graves Jr. Started in 1928 it took five years to complete. It had

a Westminster chime, perpetual calendar, split-seconds chronograph, and celestial maps. The watch had an amazing 900 single parts, 70 jewels, and weighed around 535 grams (9oz). The cost of the watch was 60,000 Swiss Francs, which today is $44,131 (£29,420).

The watch became part of the Time Museum Collection set up by Seth Attwood in Chicago during the 1970s. The watch was put up for sale at Sotheby's and achieved the highest price ever for a clock or watch, $10 million (£6.6 million). The factory was interested in buying the watch back for its own museum in Geneva, which recently opened to the public, but was outbid. This shows how strong the Patek Philippe name is today.

Patek Philippe II

After years of austerity following World War II, by the late 1950s the company was still in business, producing fine-quality watches in conservative-style cases. Its square watch (*see* below) has always been a little unusual compared with the rectangular style, which was produced in much larger numbers. Because of the lack of anything flamboyant in the company's basic design, such as interesting case lugs, the watches are on the whole quite reasonable buys as their values are not that high. They do of course all have the company's fine movements, timed in five positions and three temperatures.

In 1959 Patek Philippe decided to experiment and enter the digital watch arena with a very special prototype that used an existing movement. It added a rolling digital display that looked like a car radio. The 18ct gold case was bold, and designed in the manner of Andrew Grima who was a famous jeweller in London. This was a one-off piece and it is now in the new Patek Philippe Museum in Geneva. This is the only watch the company produced that had no hands.

Another bold project was engaging the talent of a young designer, Gilbert Albert, to give their fine watch a revolutionary new look (*see* page 91). The designs he produced are extreme and employ unconventional asymmetric triangles and rhombic forms, especially when compared with the original, simple conservative square case (as can be seen clearly with the two examples shown here). The watches he designed are highly sought-after today. They were made in platinum and yellow gold and used a similar movement to that found in the straightforward square watch. As the cases were made at different angles, the straps were specially shaped to sit square on the wrist. When these watches come up for sale the platinum models can reach as much as $37,500 (£25,000).

18ct Square Watch, 1960s

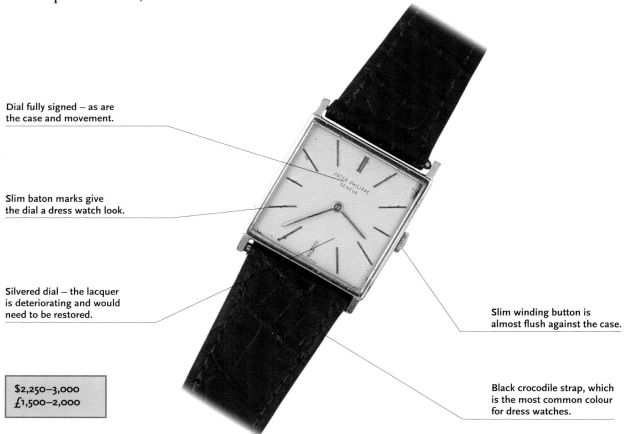

Dial fully signed – as are the case and movement.

Slim baton marks give the dial a dress watch look.

Silvered dial – the lacquer is deteriorating and would need to be restored.

Slim winding button is almost flush against the case.

Black crocodile strap, which is the most common colour for dress watches.

$2,250–3,000
£1,500–2,000

Asymmetric Watch designed by Gilbert Albert, 1960s

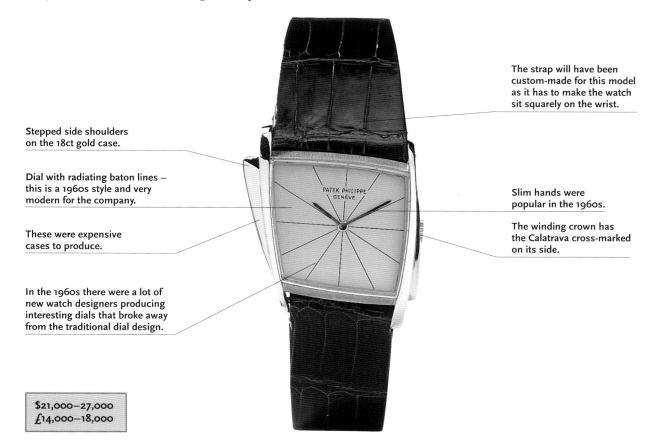

The strap will have been custom-made for this model as it has to make the watch sit squarely on the wrist.

Stepped side shoulders on the 18ct gold case.

Dial with radiating baton lines – this is a 1960s style and very modern for the company.

These were expensive cases to produce.

In the 1960s there were a lot of new watch designers producing interesting dials that broke away from the traditional dial design.

Slim hands were popular in the 1960s.

The winding crown has the Calatrava cross-marked on its side.

$21,000–27,000
£14,000–18,000

• *These fine watches are expensive to have repaired so it is best to buy only working pieces.*

• *Patek has records of all its watches, which can be traced by the date and a watch's description.*

• *Most Patek watches have solid gold buckles.*

• *Stainless steel watches are highly sought after as they are rarer than the gold examples.*

The 150th Anniversary Of Patek Philippe

The 150th-year celebration held in 1989 was planned years in advance, and to coincide with this a number of limited-edition watches were produced. These included the Officer's watch and a rarer jump-hour tonneau watch. At this time the auction market was very strong because the world economy was doing so well. There was a very special sale of vintage Patek Philippe watches organized, and this included a unique piece. It was known as Calibre 89 after the year the watch was made, and it was made specifically to increase the number of complications that could be put in a watch. This new watch had 33 complications and was a very large piece. Three examples of it were made,

in yellow, white, and pink gold. The sale did a world tour to promote this watch and the results were very good as the yellow Calibre 89 watch sold for $1.5 million (£1 million). The timing of the sale was very fortunate as just after, in the early 1990s, the economy changed with the huge stock market crash known as Black Monday.

There is now a book available on the production of the Calibre 89 and this is a collector's item in its own right. It tells the story of the massive amount of design work and skill that went into making such a piece. It also lists the staggering amount of components within the watch: 1,728 parts, 332 screws, 184 wheels, 61 bridges, 68 springs, 126 jewels, and 24 hands.

IWC: Portugieser

Although IWC still make pocket watches in small numbers, it is the wristwatches that the company is predominantly known for. This is quite ironic as it was one of the slower companies to adopt the wristwatch. However, one of IWC's most iconic designs, the Portugieser (also known as the "Portuguese"), is a wristwatch. The watch dates back to the 1930s when, according to IWC, the company "received a request from Portugal. A customer wanted a wristwatch of the same size and accuracy as a pocket watch. IWC selected the slimmest and most reliable pocket-watch movement in its range, and designed a classic stainless steel case to house it".

The result followed IWC's practice of adapting their pocket-watch movements to wristwatch cases. The Portugieser resurfaced in 1993 as a special Jubilee replica in honour of IWC's 125th anniversary. The limited Jubilee edition proved very popular as the design managed to bridge the 50-year gap without appearing remotely out of date. The Jubilee was followed in quick succession by a minute-repeater and a rattrapante (split-seconds) chronograph, which bolstered the reputation of this individual line both in terms of design and in the excellent quality of the movements.

Later still an automatic chronograph, using a highly modified Valjoux 7750 base, was introduced. Again it was the slightly eccentric design that attracted a strong following, though these watches also gained a reputation for the quality of finish under the dial.

The Portugieser was also the natural choice to house IWC's new 5000 series of movements, which have long, seven-day power reserves and Pellaton winding systems. While the chronograph is not made in limited series, IWC have still produced only a comparatively small number. However, the Portugieser 2000 has been made as a limited edition – 1,000 steel, 750 gold, and 250 in platinum – which makes it extremely sought-after by collectors already, even though it was only made at the turn of the millennium.

IWC Portugieser Automatic Chronograph, 1996

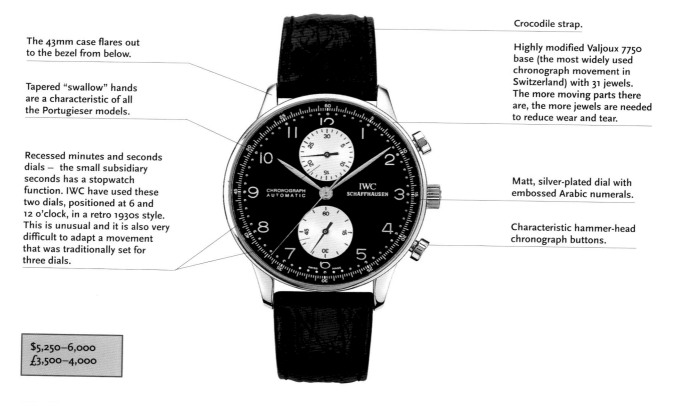

The 43mm case flares out to the bezel from below.

Tapered "swallow" hands are a characteristic of all the Portugieser models.

Recessed minutes and seconds dials – the small subsidiary seconds has a stopwatch function. IWC have used these two dials, positioned at 6 and 12 o'clock, in a retro 1930s style. This is unusual and it is also very difficult to adapt a movement that was traditionally set for three dials.

Crocodile strap.

Highly modified Valjoux 7750 base (the most widely used chronograph movement in Switzerland) with 31 jewels. The more moving parts there are, the more jewels are needed to reduce wear and tear.

Matt, silver-plated dial with embossed Arabic numerals.

Characteristic hammer-head chronograph buttons.

$5,250–6,000
£3,500–4,000

IWC Portugieser Automatic Seven-Day, 2000

Silver-plated dial with rose-gold hands and Arabic numerals.

Subsidiary seconds sub-dial at 9 o'clock, which is balanced by the power reserve dial at the 3 o'clock position.

The rose-gold case has the limited-edition number engraved on its edge.

$15,000–16,500
£10,000–11,000

▼ The Portugieser 2000 features IWC's largest automatic movement, the 5000 calibre with patented Pellaton winding system. The main barrel is capable of eight-and-a-half days' power reserve, but it has been limited by a movement stop mechanism to seven days (*see* box below).

• *The Portugieser 2000 was produced in limited numbers – 1,000 steel, 750 rose gold, and 250 platinum models.*

• *The first 100 in the series were sold as boxed sets, each with a companion steel, gold, and platinum watch with the same edition number on each watch.*

• *All the watches in this series have their limited-edition numbers engraved on the case.*

• *The automatic chronograph shown on the left is in regular production and is available with different dial colours and strap combinations.*

IWC's seven-day power reserve

One of the advantages of the relatively large size of the 5000 calibre is that IWC's engineers have been able to incorporate a power-train arrangement significantly more capable than most smaller movements. The seven-day running of the watch is based on two features that are unique to the movement.

The first is the Pellaton winding system, which connects the rotor to the barrel via a heart-shaped cam that engages a lever fork with ruby rollers at the two ends of the fork. This arrangement means that the rotor drives the barrel whichever way it is turning – about 12 rotations of the rotor equals one hour of power reserve.

The second feature is the main barrel, which contains a longer than normal spring. The barrel drum itself has some interesting characteristics, including an unusual aluminium alloy to prevent the inside of the drum from being worn down by the spring, and a high transmission ratio of barrel to centre wheel of 1:15. The total power reserve of 204 hours, or approximately eight-and-a-half days, is artificially reduced to seven days by a stop mechanism. This kicks in to prevent loss of amplitude as the spring unwinds – IWC's philosophy is that it is better to stop it early than have any inaccuracy creeping in.

Omega I

There can be little doubt that Omega are one of the most recognized and respected of the watch houses. The company has spent decades as the leading brand in an always competitive market and has a history of technical innovation and excellence. It is also riding high due to James Bond's high-profile endorsement and the launch of the Co-Axial movement.

A chink in the company's armour is the perception that Omega had a weak patch in the 1970s and early 1980s when it struggled to accommodate quartz technology into its brand values. This is not to say that Omega failed to understand the technology, as the Constellation Megaquartz 2.4MHz was the most accurate wristwatch ever made. In 1973 the watch was entered into the independent testing observatory at Neuchâtel for testing and earned the title "Marine Chronometer" after averaging just two thousandths of a second deviation per day after 63 days. But quartz movements in general production became as reliable as they were accurate, which meant that Omega's

carefully built reputation for mass-production precision was almost apparently worthless.

Putting two as seemingly opposing watches as the 1974 Megaquartz and the Marine wristwatch from 1937 up for comparison might seem a little strange. Nevertheless, these watches illustrate how a watch company's brand develops over time and how challenges have a way of re-occurring in different eras. Both watches are exercises in pure accuracy, with Omega looking to break through previously accepted barriers. Giving a wristwatch the title "Marine Chronometer" was no simple piece of branding as they were traditionally the highest-quality watches available – the accuracy of these chronometers being crucial to safe navigation at sea. Omega set out to overcome the loss of precision that came with the miniaturization of movements to fit them into wrist-watch cases. The 1937 Marine is interesting because its construction was based on the Omega Golf watch that was launched in 1931 – when closed the case is watertight and robust.

Omega Marine, 1937

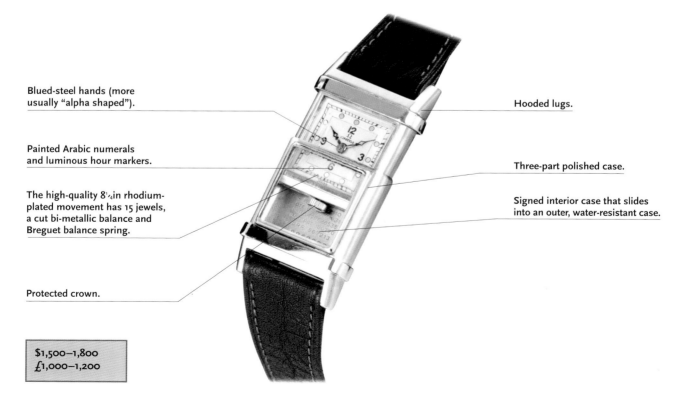

Blued-steel hands (more usually "alpha shaped").

Painted Arabic numerals and luminous hour markers.

The high-quality 8¼in rhodium-plated movement has 15 jewels, a cut bi-metallic balance and Breguet balance spring.

Protected crown.

Hooded lugs.

Three-part polished case.

Signed interior case that slides into an outer, water-resistant case.

$1,500–1,800
£1,000–1,200

Omega Megaquartz 2400, 1974

The unusual, long steel case has a bulk attenuated by two long chamfered edges, making it resemble a truncated pyramid. This is comparatively conservative in design given its date and the radical nature of the movement.

▲ Developed by Omega in collaboration with the Battele Institute of Geneva, the first prototypes were shown at the 1970 Basel Watch Fair, while mass production started in 1974. The calibre 1510's unmatched precision of one-second deviation a month was around ten times superior to that of an ordinary quartz watch. This was made possible by the tiny sealed disc resonator, which vibrates at the incredible rate of 2.4MHz.

18ct gold bezel.

Individual watch serial number set in 18ct gold on the case.

$1,800–2,250
£1,200–1,500

• *Quartz was first used as a timekeeper in 1928 by Bell Labs, and clocks with quartz oscillators slowly displaced pendulum regulator clocks as the reference standard in the 1930s and 1940s.*

• *The annual error rate of ± 12 seconds – still unbeaten precision for production wristwatch – corresponds to the rates achieved by John Harrison's first chronometers.*

Marine Chronometers

Locating longitude on the open seas was the key problem for navigators at the start of the 18th century as world trade and exploration rapidly grew. Finding longitude depended on accurate timekeeping and the current methods were clearly insufficient. The problem was finally cracked by John Harrison in 1759 with his prize-winning chronometer, H-4. By the 1800s many innovative individuals were making chronometers, including John Arnold, Thomas Mudge, and Thomas Earnshaw in England, and Ferdinand Berthoud and Pierre Le Roy in France. Although significant advances were made in chronometer production, the quality required meant that they were always made in smaller quantities than normal clocks or watches. So the term "Marine Chronometer" became the gold standard of all horology.

Typically there are several features to prevent isochronal deviation, such as a temperature-compensated balance wheel, a long power reserve (up to eight days) and indicator, and a suspension system to avoid positional errors.

Omega II

The twin requirements of strength and accuracy that dominated wartime design led directly to Omega's two main post-war watch types: the Seamaster and the Constellation. These new ranges utilized the latest self-winding (automatic) movements, which at this time had "bumper" rotors that rotated only through part of a circle and bumped against springs at each end. A small selection of Omega's Seamasters were also fitted with chronometer grade movements that offered greater accuracy. They were available with either a subsidiary seconds display or a sweep second hand. The cases had either a screw-on or snap-on back and were made in stainless steel or solid gold (pink-gold versions are rare and highly collectable). Some of the steel cases were fitted with solid gold bezels and had the lugs covered in a gold capping with a matching gold winding crown. The famous Seamaster seahorse emblem was added later to the case backs.

Alongside the Seamaster, Omega introduced the Constellation in 1952. The early models were also fitted with bumper automatics. To confirm their accuracy a special observatory emblem was marked in gold on the case backs. On later models both the emblem and the word Omega were in relief on the dial but with these very early bumper Constellations only the Omega emblem was in gold relief. Top of the range was the Grand Luxe, which was produced in a solid 18ct gold case. It had a very special "brick" bracelet and created a sensation with its 12-sided faceted "pie-pan" dial. This dial was also made out of solid 18ct gold, with the facets being machined or guilloched.

In 1956 Omega introduced a range of full 360°, full rotor, winding automatic movements. Seamaster watches were again available with either subsidiary or sweep seconds while all Constellation models had sweep seconds only. The Constellation was available with a date function at 3 o'clock using Omega's 504 movement. The Seamaster used the 490 movement with subsidiary seconds, 501 as a sweep seconds timepiece, or a 503 for a timepiece with date indication.

Omega Seamaster de Ville, 1960s

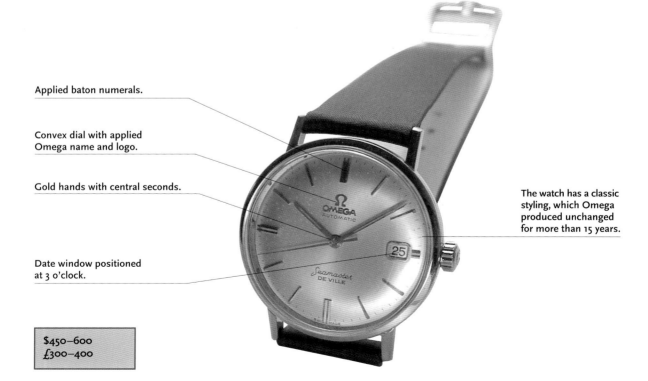

Applied baton numerals.

Convex dial with applied Omega name and logo.

Gold hands with central seconds.

Date window positioned at 3 o'clock.

The watch has a classic styling, which Omega produced unchanged for more than 15 years.

$450–600
£300–400

Omega "Pie-Pan" Constellation, 1952

Raised "Pie-Pan" dial with applied Omega logo.

Arrowhead applied hour markers.

Sword hour and minute hands with central seconds.

This crocodile strap was often replaced by the unique "brick" bracelet (now resurrected for the Co-Axial de Ville models).

Distinctive ten-sided crown.

Distinctive guilloched facets.

$750–1,050
£500–700

Incabloc shock absorber.

Bi-directional 360° winding rotor.

Swan-neck regulated balance.

Distinctive copper colour.

◄ One of the main attractions for collectors of the Constellation is the sheer quality of the movements – particularly the "Observatory" quality examples. The swan-neck regulator is there to adjust the watch time-keeping to a close rate.

Omega III

During World War II the company had supplied many thousands of watches to the British military officers and airmen. With the disposal of war supplies and the general control on imports and foreign exchange these watches started a new life. London companies such as Bravington arranged for new gold cases to be made for them by a number of English case makers. These were mainly in 9ct gold due to the cost of gold, which had risen over the war years. The movements were of high quality and not marked as government issues.

The style of these watches was similar to the regular watch shown below. It has a simple three-part case, which means it has a snap-on bezel to hold the glass, a middle case section, and a snap-on back. Such watches were produced in England for many years, right up to when Omega stopped selling watches in the 9ct-gold cases in the late 1980s.

In Europe 14ct gold is the lowest grade of metal allowed. This is often marked "585", which refers to the number of gold particles per 1,000 metal particles. The English 9ct gold only has 375 particles per 1,000. By the 1960s Omega had a large hold over the general watch market. It had become the brand to own and, as they often produced the same model in 18ct, 14ct or 9ct gold, with a gold shell and shell case, they had all the price points covered. The 9ct-gold models, such as the one shown here, had simple hand-wound movements.

The other piece shown is part of the Constellation range, which first appeared in 1952 (*see* page 124). The range was so successful that by 1958 45 per cent of all chronometers sold were Constellations. The special model has an 18ct-gold case and a cloisonné dial, which makes it highly sought-after today. These dials were produced for other companies too, such as Rolex, Patek Philippe, and Universal. Charles Poluzzi (1899–1978) was a celebrated miniaturist and enameller who created some of these special dials. As such examples are rare, watches with a Poluzzi dial will have a massively increased market value.

Regular 9ct Gold Watch, 1960s

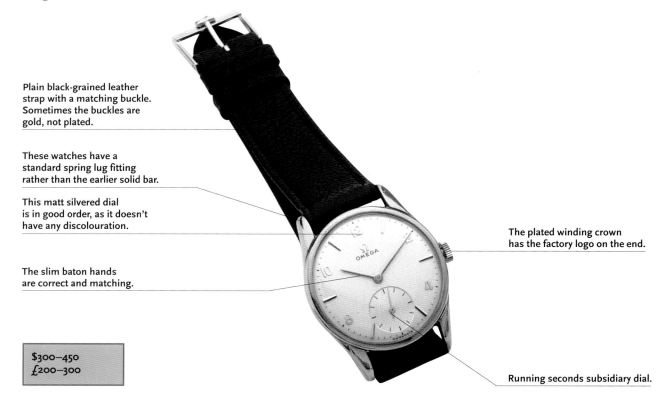

Plain black-grained leather strap with a matching buckle. Sometimes the buckles are gold, not plated.

These watches have a standard spring lug fitting rather than the earlier solid bar.

This matt silvered dial is in good order, as it doesn't have any discolouration.

The slim baton hands are correct and matching.

The plated winding crown has the factory logo on the end.

Running seconds subsidiary dial.

$300–450
£200–300

Constellation Watch with a Cloisonné Dial, 1960s

The beautiful dial centre is decorated with a classic picture of the celestial heavens. This design was also used on the case-backs of watches in the Constellation range.

The hour chapter has flamboyant raised baton marks, which are very much 1960s in style.

$12,000–18,000
£8,000–12,000

The classic solar observatory scene indicates that the watch is a chronometer-tested movement.

• *The cloisonné dial makes watches desirable, but you still need to check examples for damage as this would detract from the value considerably.*

• *Cloisonné dial watches by Universal Geneve and Omega are very rare because they were so difficult to make. They are highly desirable as collectors' items as a result.*

• *The standard 1960s Omega watches are in plentiful supply, so try to find an 18ct-model with its box, as this will make it more desirable if you sell it on at a later date.*

• *The standard 1960s watch, with the back engraved, was often given by companies to employees who were retiring. You should avoid such watches as the engraving is almost impossible to remove.*

Polychrome Enamel Dials

In the 1960s the art of expensive cloisonné dial-production was born. Watches with such dials are now some of the rarest pieces around and are also much more valuable than models without the special dial. For example, the Omega Constellation shown above would be valued at $750–1,150 (£500–700) without this dial. With top names, such as Patek Philippe and Rolex, the name is so strong that all their watches are highly collectable. They also produced unique dials, specially made to customers' orders. Other companies such as Universal and Vacheron Constantin used these cloisonné dials as well, also known as polychrome dials.

There are actually two styles of decorative enamel work. The first is champlevé. In this method the dial plate of a precious metal has its surface engraved with the outline of the design. The area within this outline is then removed before a layer of transparent or opaque enamel is put in its place.

The other method of producing this effect is cloisonné. Again the design is engraved on the dial plate but, instead of removing the metal, very fine wire is fixed to the plate to provide the outline. Then coloured enamel is placed in the compartments (*cloisons*) that have been made.

One particularly interesting enamel dial featured a map of India. This was fitted to a Rolex Oyster watch. This historic watch was once the property of the first prime minister after India's independence from the British Empire in 1947. The watch later belonged to Tenzing Norgay and was sold at auction for £202,500 (£135,000) in 2003.

Omega IV

The Omega Speedmaster is probably one of the company's most famous ranges. The first Speedmaster was created in 1957 and the range has been developed over the years. Its major claim to importance was when it was chosen by National Air Space Administration (NASA) to be its official watch. NASA needed watches for its space programme so the company bought a number of good chronograph watches and subjected them to a rigorous evaluation before selecting the Speedmaster (*see* box opposite).

The early model has a hand-wound chronograph movement and the case style is quite rounded. Later models, such as the Speedmaster MK II, have a much larger case to enable the automatic movement to be fitted. This case is made in two pieces, which is better for water resistance as there are less case parts that need to be sealed. The flat glass is made of a mineral material – this was quite new in the 1970s as earlier watches had a plastic glass. A good design feature in the later models was the placing of the tachometer scale beneath the glass, as this protects it from damage and gives the piece a clean look (on early models the scale was fitted on the outer case bezel, which made it easy to mark).

The Speedmaster 125 is an interesting watch. Made in 1973 to celebrate the company's 125th anniversary, it has a special case shape and is engraved on the back with "Speedmaster Commemorative Medal". There was a limited run of 2,000 pieces for this particular watch. The piece was also the first Speedmaster with a chronometer-rated automatic movement. Both elements mean that the watch has been highly sought-after in recent years by collectors – the special movement and rarity means that they can fetch three times the price of the MK II.

The Speedmaster made six round trips to the moon with Neil Armstrong – from his historic walk on the moon on July 21 1969 at 02:56 GMT through to the last Apollo 17 mission. Today the new Speedmaster X-33 is the standard for NASA's space shuttle missions.

Speedmaster MK II, *c.*1969

Strong, flexible link bracelet, which is made of brushed stainless steel to match the case.

The tonneau, or barrel-shaped case, is made of just two parts so there is no removable bezel.

The baton marks are luminous – this effect has been created with tritium paint, a very low-radioactive material.

The tachometer scale is protected under the mineral glass.

The subsidiary dial records the chronograph up to 30 minutes.

The brushed stainless steel effect around the case was fashionable when this watch was made.

The running seconds is not affected by the action of the chronograph and is a part of the time-of-day display.

The large winding crown has a built-in seal to prevent water getting into it.

Chronograph operating buttons: the bottom one is the reset button while the top bottom is for starting or stopping the mechanism.

$750–1,050
£500–700

Speedmaster 125, 1973

The mineral glass here is flat so there is no reflection, and the dial is very clear but is not as scratchproof as the later sapphire crystal.

The day/night indicator is useful for astronauts rotating the Earth as it gives them something to refer to for their sleep patterns.

The heavy brushed-finish stainless steel case also has a matching bracelet.

Matt black dial with very clear minute markers.

The dial is marked with "chronometer" – this was the first Speedmaster to have this movement fitted.

The sweep minute recording hand used for the chronograph has a cross on the end.

The techygraph scale, which is designed specifically for measuring speed over miles, enables the wearer to record their speed over the distance of 1 mile, up to 500 miles per hour.

$1,200–1,800
£800–1,200

• With such complicated watches repairs can be expensive so you should get a watchmaker to check over the watch to see if it is in good working order before buying.

• The Omega company has produced a number of special pieces, including the 125, and these are obviously the most desirable – and therefore the most collectable too.

• The condition of such a watch is very important – due to the age some parts may be impossible to obtain. The cases do suffer from knocks because of their thickness.

• The original Speedmaster model that went to the moon has been relaunched recently, so this might be a piece of interest to collect.

The Ultimate Test For Space Travel

In 1961 a NASA equipment-buyer went to Corrigans watch shop in Texas to purchase two each of five chronographs of different brands, including the Omega Speedmaster in order to test their suitability for space travel. Before this time astronauts wore watches of their own choosing and these included Bulova Accutron and a Speedmaster (on early missions they were worn only as back-up time-pieces). A hand-wound movement, or an automatic that could be hand-wound, could be used but automatic rotors were ineffective in zero gravity.

The ten original watches that had first arrived for testing were narrowed down to three makes – Longines, Rolex, and Omega. Using various equipment to simulate the outer-space environment, the watches were subjected to a thorough testing of their reactions to high temperature, low temperature, temperate pressure, relative humidity, oxygen atmosphere, vibration, and acoustic noise. The detailed data on how the watches performed in these conditions was collected. These tests were much harsher than any chronometer test, as the watches were also subjected to a altitude chamber that could simulate altitudes up to 110,000m (360,000ft) and a temperature range of -73°–260°C (-99.4°–500°F). A watch failed the tests if it stopped and would not restart, if the glass cracked, or the winding mechanism or push buttons failed. The results were unanimous – the Speedmaster proved to be the most reliable, so the watch was certified for all further space missions.

Heuer I

The founder of this famous company, Edouard Heuer, was 20 years old in 1860 when he decided to enter the watch world as a dealer. His firm was highly successful and he soon moved to new offices in Bienne. In about 1880 he started one of the first productions of pocket chronograph watches. Edouard died in 1892 and left his wife and five children a small fortune, which his two older sons, Jules and Charles, used to continue where their father had left off. They really expanded the range of speciality watches and, with the dawning of the age of the motor car, they produced their first dashboard timepiece in 1911. The company also produced the first 1/100th of a second timer in 1916 and had an early association with the Olympic Games as official timekeepers in the games of 1920, 1924, and 1928. The company went on to produce special stop watches for events from yacht sailing through to horse riding.

The early chronograph model shown below is a piece from the 1940s. It is known as a single-button chronograph and would have been worn by pilots as it can be operated with just one hand (the one button starts, stops, and resets the chronograph). The later, more advanced, model was called the "Carrera". It was named after the Mexican odyssey that was created in 1950 to celebrate the completion of the Panamerican highway, which linked the two hemispheres together. A race called the "Carrera Panamericana Motor Race" was started and this new watch was named after it. It was a winning design for the company, which had a massive increase in sales as a result (the company doubled its yearly turnover). Unlike the earlier model, this watch was a twin-button chronograph so the chronograph could be started and stopped at will without having to be reset. The watch is quite small in today's market – it is actually one of the most compact pieces available. It was firmly aimed at the sports car owner when first designed; the black strap with its ventilation holes echoes the look of driving gloves, which were popular at the time.

Standard 2-dial Single-button Chronograph, *c.*1940

Running seconds subsidiary dial, which is not affected by the chronograph operation.

There is a fine quarter-seconds outer scale for use with the sweeping chronograph hand.

Fixed case bars means that the straps have to be sewn on or have open ends.

The heavy leather strap was typically used on pilots watches because of its strength.

The bezel is movable and has an arrow pointer for time-elapse indication.

There is a 30-minute chronograph recording subsidiary dial.

Matt black dial with bold Arabic numerals makes the watch very clear to read.

$1,125–1,275
£750–850

Original Carrera Chronograph, *c.*1963

Broad baton marks on
a matt black ground.

Silvered inner ring
that shows the minutes.

Running seconds subsidiary
dial – this is not affected by
the chronograph operation.

Large winding crown,
which is easy to grip.

Black leather sports strap
with perforated holes to
keep the wearer's wrist cool.

The dial displays the name of
the retailer who sold the piece.

$1,800–3,000
£1,200–2,000

Rallye International Dashboard timers, *c.*1960

▶ These interesting timers
were first produced in 1933 and
continued in production until
1985. They were sold to racing
drivers who wanted to time
a car rally or track event.
They could be sold as a pair
or singularly. The nearest one
is a 60-minute timer while the
one on the far right is a long
duration timer (the elapsed
12 hours are shown in a small
aperture above the 6 o'clock
position). These pieces have
become extremely collectable in
recent years due to the interest
in motor sports, and there are
quite a number of variations
to collect (*see* page 135). Today
they fetch in the region of
$1,500–2,250 (£1,000–1,500).

Heuer II

In the 1960s Heuer purchased another watch company, Leonidas of Saint-Imier, and became Heuer-Leonidas. Over the next few years it took over the company completely (*see* page 134). With the cost of developing new products, and to secure its future, Jack Heuer decided to sell the company to its main movement-supplier, Lemania, and other shareholders.

One of Heuer's new products was a range of watches with the motorsport person in mind. With the success of the first Monaco watch, the company progressed with the Silverstone model shown below. It has more of a dress watch look with its graduated smoke dial colour but the watch was also produced with a plain red and a plain blue dial. The Silverstone Formula 1 circuit is a famous venue so, like the Carrera and Monaco watches, the Silverstone model appeals to motor-racing enthusiasts. Its design was a success and was worn by the Ferrari driver Clay Ragazzoni.

In the late 1960s the popular Monaco, one of the first automatic chronographs, was produced. It became a cult watch when Steve McQueen wore one in the classic 1970s film *Le Mans*. It is now called "Steve McQueen" by watch collectors and TAG Heuer have, in recent years, reissued this model. The new range now includes a model with a three-register dial, which can record seconds, minutes, and hours up to 12 hours.

In 1969 the successful Swiss driver Joe "Seppi" Siffert was looking for further sponsorship. As he entered the heady world of Formula 1 Jack Heuer was also looking for further exposure for his brand and Siffert was an obvious choice. Heuer became the first sponsor not from the car industry to be connected to Formula 1, and Siffert had Heuer logos on his racing overalls and on the side of the car. After Siffert sadly was killed in a racing accident, Heuer went on to sponsor other drivers – as it still does.

Silverstone Chronograph, 1974

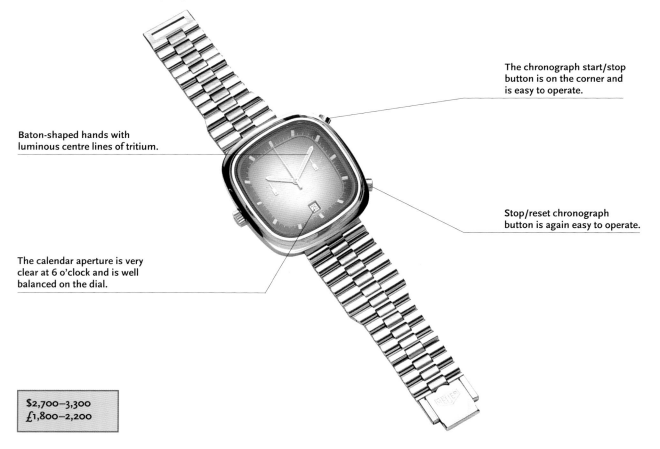

The chronograph start/stop button is on the corner and is easy to operate.

Baton-shaped hands with luminous centre lines of tritium.

Stop/reset chronograph button is again easy to operate.

The calendar aperture is very clear at 6 o'clock and is well balanced on the dial.

$2,700–3,300
£1,800–2,200

"Steve McQueen" Monaco, 1970s

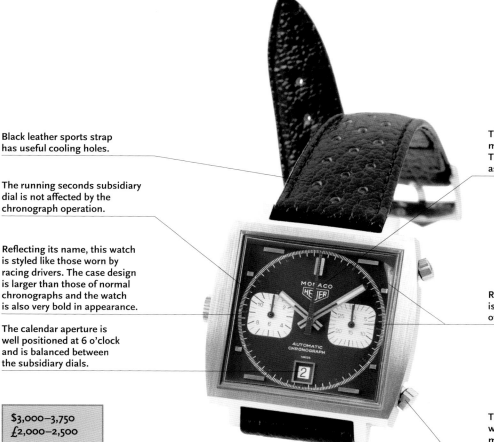

Black leather sports strap has useful cooling holes.

The running seconds subsidiary dial is not affected by the chronograph operation.

Reflecting its name, this watch is styled like those worn by racing drivers. The case design is larger than those of normal chronographs and the watch is also very bold in appearance.

The calendar aperture is well positioned at 6 o'clock and is balanced between the subsidiary dials.

$3,000–3,750
£2,000–2,500

The blue dial is signed and marked with the Monaco name. This particular dial style is known as the "Steve McQueen" Monaco.

Running seconds dial, which is not affected by the operation of the chronograph.

The chronograph reset button is well placed on the corner, which makes it easy to operate.

◄ Steve McQueen was a keen racing driver in his private life and therefore was an obvious choice for the lead roll in the film *Le Mans*. With Heuer's name on his racing overalls and on the car the film was a perfect promotion for the company. The fact that the factory has reissued the watch shows that interest in it is still there and the watches are still selling 30 years after the film was made.

Heuer III

Heuer developed a wide range of watches for all types of sporting events using different dials but the same movements. The stainless steel model shown below was not named for a specific event, but nevertheless still has a tachometer outer scale. It has been calibrated so that the miles per hour can be seen at a glance – so if a ¼ mile is done in 15 seconds then the driver is going at a speed of 60 miles per hour. Heuer produced a range of dials for wristwatches but also pocket stopwatches with high beat movements to time specific sporting events accurately including water polo, yachting, and boxing. With the introduction of new technology a lot of these pieces were deemed obsolete and were dropped from the range. This means that collectors now have a wide range of models to choose from today, and there have been special auctions purely of Heuer watches. Some of the sports stopwatch models with special dials are difficult to obtain – they must have been thrown away when the new quartz watches arrived.

The Leonidas watch company was formed in 1841 by Julien Bourquin, who chose to name his company after the legendary king of Sparta. The company developed all aspects of short-time measurement mechanisms for stopwatches and chronographs. With the growth in the aviation business it started supplying dashboard clocks and instrument panel clocks. It was therefore a good choice of company for Heuer to link up with, and in 1964 they joined to create Heuer-Leonidas SA. There was a crossover in the range of the two companies. Leonidas' Easy Rider watch came in a choice of bright plastic cases. It was produced for the youth market and had a less expensive movement called a pin pallet. The model called the "Jacky Ickx Easy Rider", sold by Heuer, was named after the famous Belgian racing driver. The watch was produced in various brightly coloured plastic cases as well as metal. Leonidas' Easy Rider watches do not have the same interest level or value to collectors as the Heuer model, so are worth about 50 per cent less.

Stainless Steel Chronograph, *c.*1970

The dial has a tachometer scale for recording speeds over a one-mile distance.

The running seconds subsidiary dial is not affected by the chronograph operation.

The fine baton hands have black lines down their centres to give them a 1970s style look.

The calendar aperture is very well placed and balanced on the dial.

The padded leather strap gives the piece a "sporty" feel.

The chronograph operating buttons – the start/stop is on the top and the reset at the bottom.

There is a 30-minute recording device for the chronograph mechanism.

$450–750
£300–500

Jacky Ickx Easy Rider, *c.*1970

Flyback chronograph hand – make sure that the function still operates properly.

The dials were available in different colours – always check that they are in good condition.

The sports plastic strap is typical of this period.

The all-important signature of Jacky Ickx.

The tachometer scale has been mounted on the bezel and is used to calculate speeds.

$750–1,200
£500–800

- *The Easy Rider watches came with three different coloured dials – red, white, and black. Whatever the colour, only the Jacky Ickx models have true value.*

- *Watches with plastic cases must not have any damage as this would be impossible to repair.*

- *Make sure the watch you are considering buying is running and, if possible, complete with its box and paperwork as these will add extra value.*

- *Stainless steel watches can be re-finished as the brushed stainless steel becomes polished over the years, which dulls the effect of the graining.*

Dashboard Chronographs

Since Heuer was founded the company have developed a range of special timers, clocks, and sports timers. Of highest collecting interest are the car dashboard timers, which have names such as Master Time, Autavia, Super Autavia, Monte Carlo, and Sebring. The first models were produced in 1933 and called the "Autavia" – the name is a mixture of "Automobiles" and "Aviation". They had black dials and could record up to 12 hours. The pieces were first sold as single stop-watches, then a time-of-day clock called the Master Time appeared, which could be mounted next to the Autavia on the base plate supplied by Heuer. Over the years watch retailers created their own Rally Masters by

taking a Master Time and Monte Carlo and mounting them together. The Monte Carlo name replaced Autavia as the name of these clocks. The Monte Carlo had a 12-hour stop-watch, with the hours being recorded in a small aperture. This model first appeared in 1958. The Autavia name was not completely lost and was later transferred to a wrist chronograph watch. A black-finish case replaced the chrome finish in the mid-1950s and the plastic case was used from the 1970s up to the end of production in 1985. These dashboard chronographs then became redundant as quartz was more accurate and could do everything the chronographs did at a fraction of the cost.

Heuer: Monza

Monza is one of Italy's oldest racing circuits and is famous all over the world. Constructed in 1922 by the Milan Automobile Club, the circuit was built to mark the 25th anniversary of the club's foundation. Heuer's Monza chronograph watch followed a line of successful motor racing watches that were each associated to a legendary racing circuit, such as Monaco, Carrera, and Targa Florio.

The first new Monza watch was an automatic chronograph in a curved, cushion-shaped case. The movements on the first series of watches were not chronometer-rated and did not have the fast beat movements. The calibre 36 appeared in 2002 and was launched by the company that by now called itself TAG Heuer. On earlier watches in the historic range the dials are marked "Heuer" but this had now changed to say "TAG Heuer". The name change occurred when "Techniques d'Avant-Garde" acquired a majority stake in the company in 1985. The company was then floated on the stock market and, in 1999, was bought by the French luxury produce company LVMH for almost 1.2 billion Swiss Francs ($0.68 billion).

Heuer was not the easiest name to pronounce so the addition of "TAG" was welcomed and has been well branded over the years. When TAG Heuer was put up for sale it was only the watch side of TAG that was sold, but as the name is so well known it was kept.

The newly produced version of the Monza watch uses the company's finest movement, the Cal 36. This is a chronometer-rated movement that has been specially decorated with Côtes de Genève – a vertically striped pattern that is visible to the wearer by the inclusion of a transparent back to the case. The silver dialled models have sectors of guilloche engraving, which gives the watered silk look that was popular in the 1930s. This new range of Monzas also includes non-chronograph watches that are housed in the same cushion-shaped case but are cheaper to purchase.

Monza Classic, 2001

The curved sapphire crystal gives a very clear dial view and cannot be scratched.

Running seconds subsidiary dial is not affected by the chronograph operation.

The very clear chronograph flyback hand has an arrow-shaped end.

Stainless steel case; it has brushed sides and a bright finish.

$3,000–3,750
£2,000–2,500

▲ The watch has a Breguet-style faceted winding crown, which reflects the sporting spirit of the 1930s. The twin start/stop chronograph operating buttons flank the dial. There is also a fine outer chapter divided into quarter seconds, and the polished-steel pierced hands are nicely shaped and have white infields.

Monza Cal 36, 2003

Black dial with a fine outer seconds scale. The dial is marked "calibre 36" – this special movement can record up to one-tenth of a second.

The hands are different on the flyback and subsidiary dials.

Well-padded crocodile strap provides the perfect finishing touch for this special watch.

▼ The Cal 36 is beautifully finished with a damascened nickel movement that is visible to the owner as the case has a crystal back. The self-winding rotor is also visible and is fully signed by the maker. The balance wheel can be seen at 12 o'clock – this beats at 36,000 rates per hour, from which the movement gets its name.

$5,100–5,400
£3,400–3,600

• *The first editions of the Monza are not fitted with Cal 36 movements so they do not have the crystal case back. Both the models shown here are still in production – the Cal 36 costs so much more to purchase because of the movement's high quality.*

• *There is a limited-edition Monza in 18ct rose gold, which is fitted with the Cal 36 movement. This is a collector's model and it comes with a special wooden box and eye glass to enable the owner to examine the movement in detail.*

The Cal 36 and Chronometer Tests

In the Cal 36 the balance wheel vibrates at a massive 36,000 swings per hour. As most watches have balances that move at 18,000 per hour this is twice the action (the higher it is the more accurate a timer the movement is). As the watch is a chronometer and a chronograph the construction and tolerances of the movement have to be much closer so that the watch does not perform any differently with the additional chronograph mechanism (this creates additional friction for the watch to work with). The movement is beautifully finished and the owner can view it through its crystal back. It has 31 jewels to reduce the friction and these make the piece a joy to look at.

The term chronometer can be used only when the watch has passed a thorough testing period by the COSC (Contrôle Officiel Suisse des Chronometres). This body individually tests each movement over a period of 15 days and nights at three different temperatures (23°C, 38°C, and 8°C/73.4°F, 100.4°F, and 46.4°F). The variation of the movements must have a mean time range of -4 to +4 seconds per day to be called a chronometer, which would mean the watch has a 99.99 degree of precision. This is the highest precision rate a mechanical movement can achieve.

Rolex I

During the 1920s the Rolex watch company made no attempt to enter the automatic wristwatch market. Harwood was the main producer of these and had a number of patented ideas, which somewhat restricted development by other companies. However, this all changed when Harwood went bankrupt in 1929. Rolex had already designed the Oyster case in 1927, which was fully waterproof. Hans Wilsdorf, the founder of Rolex, knew that if the necessity of setting and winding this watch daily could be removed the watch could be even more popular. So in the early 1930s the company started to design a self-winding movement, in which a rotor is moved 360 degrees. This is a better solution than one that incorporates a buffer rotor as that sends shock waves through the movement. The Rolex self-winding mechanism was also silent, unlike all others before it. But the design had one main disadvantage: for the motor to be able to move 360 degrees the watch had to be a lot thicker. The case back was therefore very domed in shape and became known as the "Bubble Back". The watch was launched in 1934 but was a slow seller – with the world Depression still present the automatic watch was still seen by Swiss watch companies as no more than a novelty. However, the new self-winding chronometer movement brought a new accuracy to wristwatches and had a long production run up to the 1950s. This means that there are a lot of watches for collectors to choose from.

The bicolour Hooded Bubble Back was introduced in 1941 but was not as popular as the normal Bubble model. The hooded part of the name refers to the infilled section across the case shoulder. The lack of sales when it was first made has resulted in the fact that this watch is rather more desirable to collectors today and so fetches more than the regular Bubble Back.

Regular Bubble Back, *c.*1938

These watches were made in a number of metals so check inside the case back for the quality of the gold.

Smooth bezel. A later model, which came out in the 1940s, had a milled bezel. Worn bezels are best left alone as restoration can affect the value.

Pierced blued-steel hands with luminous painted infills.

Centre seconds hand. The earlier model also had a small seconds hand.

Screw-down crowns do wear out but can be restored or replaced. These Bubble Back watches are no longer waterproof due to their age.

Check the case shoulders for dents or bad marks as they may be difficult to remove.

$2,700–3,300
£1,800–2,200

Bicolour Hooded Bubble Back, 1945

This is the hood that fills the space – on non-hooded models there is a gap between the case and strap.

The bezels also came with an engraved surround with hour marks. Always try to buy a watch with a non-worn bezel.

The Rolex sprung bracelet was one of the first made for a sports watch. The springs do break but can be replaced by a specialist watchmaker.

The dial is in good order and has the added interest of the retailer's name, which was South American. This history makes it more desirable.

The gold cap on the crown has been broken. These can be replaced as spares are available.

$3,750–5,250
£2,500–3,500

▶ The hooded case first came out in the 1940s but was not that popular at the time. The hands are of a different style to the regular Bubble Back and there is no luminous paint infill.

• *The Bubble Back watch had a long production-run so there is a large supply from which to choose.*

• *The backs of such watches have milled edges – check that these have not been damaged.*

• *There are plenty of fakes of this watch around so always buy from a good source (for example, sometimes the plain models have been converted to look like the hooded model).*

• *An unrestored dial is more collectable as long as it is in good order.*

The Founder of Rolex

Hans Eberhard Wilhelm Wilsdorf was born in Kulmbach, a tiny village in Bavaria, Germany, on March 22 1881. Both his parents died while he was still young and he was sent to boarding school where he excelled at maths and languages. On leaving school he worked for a company in Geneva buying and selling pearls. This provided him with good experience of negotiating with clients all around the world. Hans had seen the watch industry in Switzerland and watched with interest the development of smaller movements and their increased industrial production. He spent some of his spare time with a watchmaker and this helped him decide that this

was the area that he wanted to move into. After moving to London in 1903 he set up a business with Alfred James Davis, who financed their new venue, called Wilsdorf & Davis. They began importing movements from Switzerland and had the cases made in London. These were stamped with "W&D". Wilsdorf began to understand the importance of having a company name that was universal the world over, and realized that the trade name should be short and incapable of being misspelt. How he arrived at the word Rolex is unclear, but it was first registered in 1908 in Geneva and has since become one of the most recognized names in the world.

Rolex II

From its earliest days Rolex had a goal to produce an effective watchproof watch and the Oyster was the highly successful result. The patented screw-down winding crown is fine for swimming but the pressure on the watch case is quite small. Diving watches must be of far stronger and heavier construction. During World War II Rolex did supply a jumbo stainless Oyster case to the Panerai for use by Italian military frogmen but they were very large and never sold to the civilian market (until recently).

The 1950s saw the growth of diving as a sport and the development of the compressed air diving system. Rolex was quick to recognize the importance of having an accurate way of measuring time under water and the first Submariner was launched in 1954 at the Swiss Watch Fair. These first watches were pressure-tested to 100m (330ft) and had winding crowns without protective guards. The early models are known by

collectors as "James Bond" watches because they were worn in the first four James Bond films. By the 1960s the watch had improved with the addition of guards to the crown and a thicker case, which meant it could go down to a depth of 200m (660ft). The 1972 model was used by Roger Moore in the 1973 Bond film *Live and Let Die*. This was converted to accommodate all the various additional functions James Bond needed! It had a hyper-intensified magnetic field powerful enough to deflect bullets even at a long range and the rotating bezel could be turned into a saw. This effect was created by blowing air down a small pipe to turn vanes in the case. One of the most dramatic moments of the film was when James Bond was about to be lowered into a pool of hungry sharks and he used the watch to cut himself free from the rope that he was tied up with. This moment of watch "magic" has helped to make the Submariner so collectable today.

Standard Submariner, 1960s

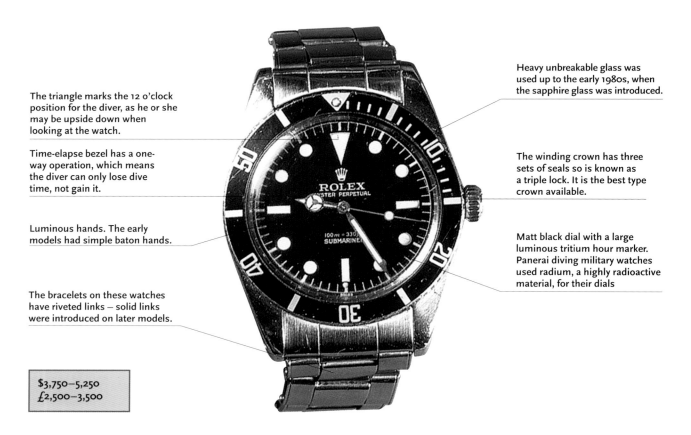

The triangle marks the 12 o'clock position for the diver, as he or she may be upside down when looking at the watch.

Time-elapse bezel has a one-way operation, which means the diver can only lose dive time, not gain it.

Luminous hands. The early models had simple baton hands.

The bracelets on these watches have riveted links – solid links were introduced on later models.

Heavy unbreakable glass was used up to the early 1980s, when the sapphire glass was introduced.

The winding crown has three sets of seals so is known as a triple lock. It is the best type crown available.

Matt black dial with a large luminous tritium hour marker. Panerai diving military watches used radium, a highly radioactive material, for their dials

$3,750–5,250
£2,500–3,500

Early "James Bond Live and Let Die" Submariner, 1960s

The time-elapse bezel moves one way only, so that the dive time cannot be increased by accident.

The case on these models is much stronger than on earlier pieces, which means the watches can go much deeper.

The winding button is flanked by very strong protective guards to stop it from being knocked off.

Matt black dial with discoloured luminous markers. Collectors like to keep the aged look rather than restoring such examples.

On the bezel there is a luminous dot within the triangle, which marks the end of the dive time.

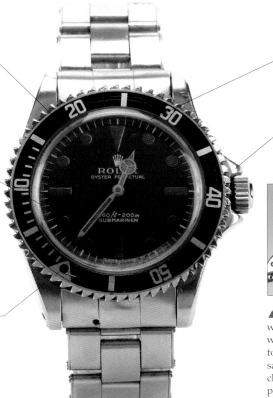

▲ This view shows the small holes that were made in the case of James Bond's watch to allow the the fine operated lines to create the visual effects of the spinning saw bezel and the numerals on the dial changing when the watch become a powerful magnet.

► A scene from *Live and Let Die* showing Roger Moore and Jane Seymour. James Bond watches have been the perfect product placement for the various companies who have supplied them. Watches do not normally have such a large role in films, but in the James Bond movies they provide the hero with many of his means of escape through the various gadgets hidden within them. Omega Seamaster are currently producing watches for the James Bond films. The company has produced a limited edition of the Seamaster – 10,007 pieces for the 40th anniversary of James Bond. These are likely to be of interest in the future.

$45,000–60,000
£30,000–40,000

Rolex III

In its early days Rolex did not have a lot to do with the chronograph, preferring to leave it to other companies while it focused on the waterproof Oyster case, which was its major success in the 1930s. It was not until 1937 that Rolex started making a number of chronographs, which had a single-button operation start/stop and reset. The best-known Rolex chronograph is called the "Cosmograph". This was not the first watch to be called by this name, as it was originally used on a short-lived model that had stars and a moon on the dial. However, Rolex kept the name and used it on its new chronograph, which was launched in 1960. The first of these Cosmographs was produced with simple push pieces for the chronograph, but there were incidents of button-seals breaking when they were operated underwater, and later examples have screw-down buttons as a result.

The most interesting model to the collector is the "Paul Newman" Daytona. This model was nicknamed by Italian collectors after Paul Newman wore the watch in a photoshoot for the cover of an Italian magazine. The exotic Daytona dials were available in black with white subsidiary dials, or cream with black subsidiary dials, and used a different typeface as well as the small square markers on the dial, and a red outer minute scale. The exotic dial of the cosmograph sells at a premium over the standard dial pieces as this is one of Rolex's most distinctive designs, and the watch is of a size that means it can be worn by women as well as men. The later, standard model from the 1980s, shown below, has a silvered dial that is much plainer in style, but the case has now been fitted with the screw-down chronograph pushers. The watches were available with various bezels and some came with a plastic insert for a different look. This was also available with the exotic dial but after the mid-1960s this particular dial was no longer made. Today there are also a number of expensive diamond-set Cosmographs that are particularly popular in the Middle East.

Daytona, 1980s

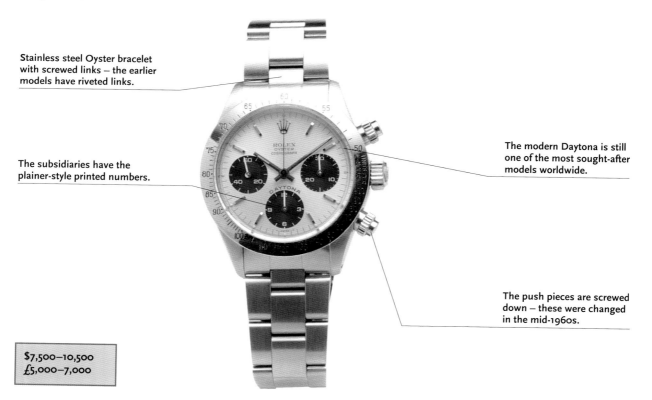

Stainless steel Oyster bracelet with screwed links – the earlier models have riveted links.

The subsidiaries have the plainer-style printed numbers.

The modern Daytona is still one of the most sought-after models worldwide.

The push pieces are screwed down – these were changed in the mid-1960s.

$7,500–10,500
£5,000–7,000

Paul Newman Daytona, 1960s

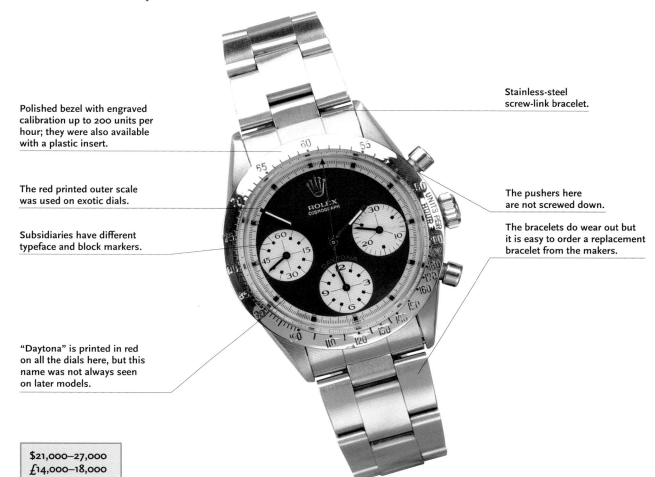

Polished bezel with engraved calibration up to 200 units per hour; they were also available with a plastic insert.

The red printed outer scale was used on exotic dials.

Subsidiaries have different typeface and block markers.

"Daytona" is printed in red on all the dials here, but this name was not always seen on later models.

Stainless-steel screw-link bracelet.

The pushers here are not screwed down.

The bracelets do wear out but it is easy to order a replacement bracelet from the makers.

$21,000–27,000
£14,000–18,000

- *The exotic dials are the most collectable. However, there are very good re-finished examples about, so always buy from a good source because having the original finish is a large part of a watch's value.*

- *Repairing one of these watches should not be a problem so long as water has not caused damage.*

- *All the models up to the late-1980s have hand-wound movements as the automatic didn't come out until 1991.*

- *A stainless steel model with an exotic dial is valued at almost the same as an 18ct model that has a plain dial.*

The Daytona Excitement

The Rolex Cosmograph was never a big seller as it was only a hand-wound watch and not as popular as the GMT or Explorer models. In 1986 the sales of this watch were lagging behind Rolex's other models, but a demand suddenly appeared for it that marked the start of the watch's rise to stardom. Italian dealers started buying Cosmographs from Great Britain and the USA after seeing Paul Newman photographed on a magazine cover with the watch. The stainless steel watches have been the most sought-after, and prices rose from a low $1,400 (£930) in the mid-1980s to $7,000 (£4,600) in the mid-'90s

and, at the height of the craze, an 18ct-gold Paul Newman model sold for $35,000 (£23,000). In 1991 Rolex released the new Daytona. The steel model is the most difficult to buy as there is a six-year waiting list for it. Many people buy the watch to make a profit, and the steel version is most popular because it is rarer (Rolex make more money from selling the gold and mixed-metal watches). Recently two 1979 prototypes of a Cosmograph appeared at an auction sporting Ferrari-red dials. These had never been seen before and fetched over $300,000 (£200,000) each.

Rolex IV

The 1960s Oyster Precision Royal is a hand-wound watch and was one of the company's most affordable watches. It has a dress-watch look with its interesting applied gilt batons but a sports watch construction. The watches were made in large numbers and have changed over the years – now the Airking is the starting-price piece (*see* page 148). Rolex stopped making the hand-wound Oyster a few years ago, but in its time this watch was popular in the general market.

The Explorer range was produced out of the strong and reliable Bubble Back watches (*see* page 138), which had gained a good reputation. This was the obvious choice on which to base the new mountaineers' and expedition watch, and field trials were arranged to test it out. It is generally accepted that the watch was made to honour the historic assent of Mount Everest in 1953 by Edmund Hillary and Tenzing Norgay. The very first Explorers used the Bubble Back case with a special dial, but the model progressed to using a slimmer Oyster case. The Airking is a dress watch Oyster with a smaller case-size – these were not popular among collectors when they first came out as they were unfamiliar and people thought they were fakes, but with the current interest in Explorers there are cases of Explorer dials being put on Airking cases so you need to be wary of this. Fortunately Rolex hold records of all its watches and dial types, so collectors can confirm with the company that a watch's case number and model reference is correct before buying it.

In 1989 Rolex withdrew the Explorer from its range, to the amazement of Rolex dealers as it was the model in longest production, having been made from 1963 to 1989. The new, revamped model arrived six months later and had a solid link rather than a folded bracelet, sapphire glass, and a new case. The new dial has white-gold skeleton numerals filled with luminous tritium filling; the only thing it shares with the old piece is the classic hands. New models are also hard to find as the sports Rolex models are the most sought-after.

Oyster Precision Royal, *c.*1960

Oyster folded link-bracelet with riveted links.

The black dial has never been that popular apart from on sports watches, but its combination with the gilt numerals here make for an interesting design.

The screw-down buttons on these do wear as the crown is unscrewed every day for winding (but they can be replaced).

The Oyster case has a screw back with a milled edge – check that it has not been damaged as this would devalue the watch.

Polished bezel with a plastic glass – these are easily replaced when necessary.

$750–1,050
£500–700

ROLEX
OYSTER
ROYAL

PRECISION

Rolex Explorer, *c.*1969

Black is the only colour used on Explorer dials. The dial ages with time and this makes the watch more collectable.

Plastic glasses were fitted up to the 1990s, which is when the sapphire glass was first fitted.

The plain polished bezel was the only style to be fitted on this watch.

Oyster cases are very strong and can be repolished but dents may be difficult to remove.

The Mercedes hand and large luminous marks make the dial visible in poor light conditions.

Screw-down crown with the Rolex mark on it.

The cases have screw-on backs.

$2,700–3,300
£1,800–2,200

• *The dials develop a faded look with age and the luminous hand and batons start to yellow.*

• *The earlier Explorer models used the large Bubble Back case but this was changed to the Airking case in the mid-1950s.*

• *Check with Rolex if you want to make sure that your watch has its correct Explorer dial.*

• *The Oyster Royal is one of the least expensive watches so there is a large choice to collect, and many variations.*

The Rarest Rolex "Kew A" Watches

Rolex was one of the first watch manufacturers that produced chronometer-rated watches (*see* page 137) and these pieces were supplied with their own rating sheets. Up until the 1940s the watch cases were also marked inside with the number of world records the watches had achieved in timing competitions. This engraving was a good advertising tool for the company.

In 1947 Rolex decided to see if they could produce some watches that would pass the ultimate six-week test at the National Physical Laboratory, Teddington, England to win a "Kew A" certificate (this test originated from the mid-19th century). They decided

to submit 140 watches for the trials. The movements of these were custom-made, and had a bimetallic brass balance wheel with very fine balance pivots of only seven-hundredths of a millimetre, matched with a free-sprung Nivarox alloy Breguet over-coil spring.

Out of the batch of 145 watches submitted only nine failed to receive the acclaimed "Kew A" rating. Teddington stopped performing this watch-testing in the early 1950s. These watches have become very collectable in recent years as the history adds to their interest. When they appear, steel-case examples can fetch $4,500–6,000 (£3,000-4,000) and gold-case watches $12,000–15,000 (£8,000–10,000).

Rolex V

The origins of the Explorer model dates back over 50 years (*see* page 144). The watch came to the world's attention when it was used for the Sir John Hunt-led successful expedition of the ascent of Everest in 1953. The watch was used by members of the team and proved to be capable of standing up to such harsh conditions. The watch became a big success and was called the Explorer I. The new updated Explorer II, based on the company's GMT watch, was launched in 1971. This is a larger watch with a fixed outer-engraved 24-hour bezel marking the hours of daylight and darkness. The large orange hand gives the watch a 1970s feel. The watch was difficult to sell but has enjoyed renewed interest recently. This may be due the resurgence of 1970s style in general. The watch was withdrawn from sale in the mid-1980s and replaced six months later with a new watch with a sapphire glass, a new bezel design, and the typical Mercedes hands. This was available with a choice of black or white dial. The white dial models have become a favourite among collectors as the paint has a habit of fading, and turns from bright white to a pale ivory – this is especially attractive next to the white-gold hands and hour markers. The company now uses a non-fade paint for its white dials. The modern watches are difficult to purchase at the moment at retail price as Rolex sports models are in high demand. This means the watches are being sold more through non-Rolex agents as collectors' watches.

The Explorer has always been thought of as a watch that can survive any hazards or conditions thrown at it, and this is reflected in its name. All Explorers have the classic hands that collectors call "Mercedes" for convenience – the correct name is in fact "skelette", or skeleton, hands. The 24-hour feature was originally for cave explorers, who, Rolex claim, soon lose all notion of time. This must have created a very limited market! However, the use of the 24-hour clock is much more common now so the Explorer is also useful for pilots and other such people today.

Modern Rolex Explorer II, 2003

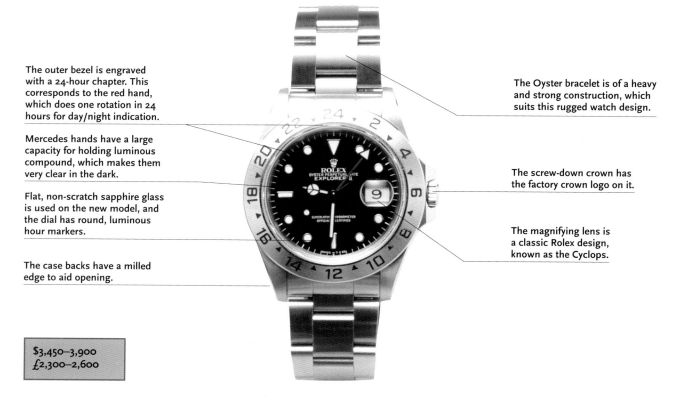

The outer bezel is engraved with a 24-hour chapter. This corresponds to the red hand, which does one rotation in 24 hours for day/night indication.

Mercedes hands have a large capacity for holding luminous compound, which makes them very clear in the dark.

Flat, non-scratch sapphire glass is used on the new model, and the dial has round, luminous hour markers.

The case backs have a milled edge to aid opening.

The Oyster bracelet is of a heavy and strong construction, which suits this rugged watch design.

The screw-down crown has the factory crown logo on it.

The magnifying lens is a classic Rolex design, known as the Cyclops.

$3,450–3,900
£2,300–2,600

Orange Hand Explorer II, 1985

This dial has a much busier layout, with a 24-hour bezel, minutes, and hours to look at; the more recent dial (below left) is much easier to read.

The plastic glass is unbreakable but will scratch.

This has a similar fixed 24-hour engraved surround to the modern example, and a large orange hand.

The winding button is protected by twin case-guards in the same way that diving models' buttons are.

This has the same classic magnifying lens on the date.

$6,000–9,000
£4,000–6,000

- Rolex supplied various expeditions with their watches, and some have engraved backs that indicate this. Such examples are rare and would command a premium today.

- The bezels do sometimes get quite worn on the early models so try to purchase a watch with a crisp bezel.

- Later models, with sapphire glasses, are very expensive to replace – around four times the cost of plastic glass – so check the condition for chips or scratches before buying.

The Rolex Marketing Machine

From the very first Oyster watch, Hans Wilsdorf understood the value of presenting his product and worked hard to gain publicity from England's national press. In 1927 Wilsdorf decided to hold back all the company's yearly advertising budget to buy the front page of the *Daily Mail*. The advert read "Make it a Rolexmas" and was placed in time for Christmas. The advert also publicized the attempt by the first Englishwoman, Mercedes Gleitz, to swim the English Channel. She did this in 15 hours and the Oyster watch she was wearing also performed well. She kept this historic watch but it recently appeared at a London auction and was sold by one of her descendants for $24,000 (£16,000). Wilsdorf gained further publicity by giving the Swiss water-polo team Oyster watches. This practise continues today, and many top golfers and other famous people such as classical musicians are associated with Rolex watches. In 1986 the Stegar international Polar expedition was supplied with Explorer II watches, which came with cloth straps so they could be worn over bulky clothing. By continuing to supply such people with its watches Rolex gains more publicity than money could buy, and is also given the opportunity to prove how reliable its models are in all circumstances.

Rolex VI

The Rolex Airking was born in the late 1950s out of the large Bubble Back watch. This new watch no longer had a raised back and was a slimmer piece than its predecessors. It became the first level automatic and was also available with the date aperture. Today it is the most reasonable watch in the current range and comes in stainless steel. The current watches have sapphire glass fitted, which is much stronger and clearer to view than the plastic glass previously used.

The other watch shown here is a famous Milgauss, which is probably one of the least available watches ever made. The timekeeping rate on all watches can be affected by high magnetic fields. To protect the Milgauss mechanism from this, Rolex placed it in a soft iron shield. This watch was created in 1954 specifically for the people working in power stations or on scientific experiments. The name Milgauss comes from *gausse*, which is the unit measurement of magnetic fields, and *mille*, the French word meaning 1,000. The first watches had a Submariner bezel with a honeycomb dial, large luminous dots, and the Milgauss name in red. Only a very small number of these watches were produced. The next model was made with its own dedicated bezel and a new dial.

The Milgauss was never a great seller as it was aimed at a small professional market of buyers who needed the anti-magnetic features (although some people did buy it purely because they liked the larger case). The model was withdrawn from the Rolex catalogue in 1988 but continued to be available by special order. Today, because of its rarity in terms of numbers sold, the watch is rated very highly on the collectors' wanted list. One of the most interesting models was the fourth series. Produced in the 1950s, the watch has an unusual centre seconds hand shaped to resemble a classic lightning bolt; as the watch has an electrical connection this is very appropriate. This model is one of the most interesting pieces, and an important watch for any serious collector of this field.

Oyster Airking, 2003

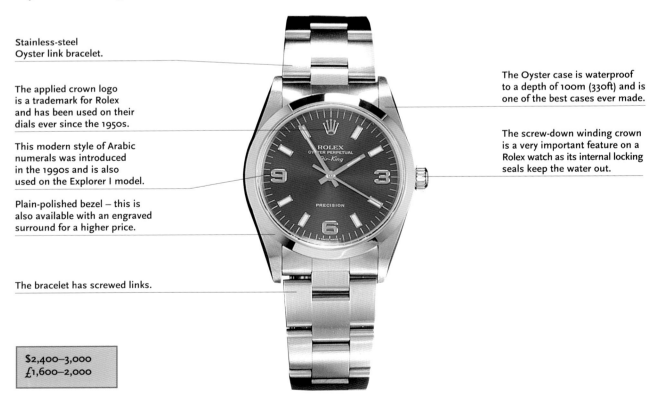

Stainless-steel Oyster link bracelet.

The applied crown logo is a trademark for Rolex and has been used on their dials ever since the 1950s.

This modern style of Arabic numerals was introduced in the 1990s and is also used on the Explorer I model.

Plain-polished bezel – this is also available with an engraved surround for a higher price.

The bracelet has screwed links.

The Oyster case is waterproof to a depth of 100m (330ft) and is one of the best cases ever made.

The screw-down winding crown is a very important feature on a Rolex watch as its internal locking seals keep the water out.

$2,400–3,000
£1,600–2,000

Milgauss, 1968

Plain, polished bezel used on the seconds series of watches in the early 1960s.

The applied baton makers on the dial are very similar to those on the early Airking dials. These age very well due to the lack of watch damage (they are protected by the Oyster case).

The dial is marked to indicate that the movement has been chronometer-rated.

This Oyster bracelet also has screwed links.

The bracelet is wider than that used on the Airking.

Screwed-down winding crown with the crown logo on the end.

The flat aluminium hands have luminous strips down their centres. The earlier examples used anti-magnetic alloy hands.

These dials were available in black or silver.

$10,500–13,500
£7,000–9,000

Rare Milgauss

▶ This watch, with its honeycomb dial and arrowhead markers, is from the earliest series. This used the bezel from a Submariner (by the 1960s the bezel was replaced with the plain one seen above). This example is shown on a non-Rolex strap but it would originally have come with the Oyster link bracelet. This change does not affect the value as bracelets are often changed. $18,000–22,500 (£12,000–15,000)

Rolex VII

In its early days the Rolex watch company had a number of watches marketed under other names, such as Unicorn and Rolco. These were Oyster-cased watches, often in nickel-plate with standard movements. These were aimed at the lower end of the market. The other names were dropped and today it is the Tudor watch, which has been around since 1945, that is the least expensive model. It has the excellent Oyster case but uses a different movement with fewer jewels than the normal Rolex mechanism.

The early Tudor watches were overlooked by collectors but have now gained interest among new collectors. The models are often similar in looks to the chronograph. The day/date is in stainless steel, whereas the Rolex model's is in 18ct gold or platinum only, which results in a major price difference. The other model produced as a Tudor is the Tudor Cosmograph, and this has become very popular in the USA and Japan. It has a five-year waiting list to buy new, and has also been taken up by collectors.

The Rolex watch has such a reputation that companies often add their own logos or pictures in order to promote themselves (*see* below right). They have also become popular retirement presents. The Eaton paper company often used Rolex watches in order to promote itself. In the 1930s the Rolex Prince watch was a popular present to give its employees and was known as the "quarter-century club watch" because it was used to celebrate an employee's 25 years with the company (nowadays TVs and other goods are much more common retirement gifts). The numbers were replaced on the dial with figures spelling out "¼ Century Club", and the Rolex name was replaced with "Eaton". These models often now have their dials changed back to the standard design. In fact this has happened so often that the original Eaton watches are now collectable. There are also reproduction quarter-century dials being made. These dials were also used on gold Oyster presentation watches. They all have a custom engraving on their backs and in the 1980s, with a boom in prices, a lot of the Prince watches appeared on the wrist-watch market.

Other clients, such as Middle Eastern Royal, also used Rolex watches as presents for their guests. Examples of its customized watches have the Royal crest on the dials. These do come up for sale but do not fetch great prices as they were given away in larger numbers, so are far more readily available.

Tudor Oyster Watch, 1972

Stainless-steel bracelet. Look for wear between the links as this is where the bracelet is particularly vulnerable.

Brightly polished bezel holding the plastic glass. Most light marks that have occurred to bezels can be polished out.

The dial is in good order, as on most Oysters, as the case is so good at stopping water damage.

Bracelet end-pieces are folded down to clamp to the case. These may become loose over the years but can be tightened.

The back has a milled edge so that a case tool can be used to remove it when necessary.

$750–1,050
£500–700

Rolex Oyster, 1960s

These watches are normally fitted on a steel bracelet as the straps shown here are not waterproof.

Brightly finished bezel with plastic glass.

The dial is badly discoloured due to the lacquer breaking down and the silver oxidizing; however, this can be restored.

$450–750
£300–500

Calendar aperture under the famous Cyclops lens.

The Precision is the most simple Oyster watch that Rolex produce.

Promotional Dials

► Companies such as Coca-Cola and Disney have added logos to Rolex watches in order to advertise or to customize the watches to give them as gifts to employees. The addition here of the Disney cartoon figure Mickey Mouse would add significant value as it brings the watch above the thousands of standard examples that are around. The watch would fetch about $1,500–2,250 (£1,000–1,500).

Other watch companies have produced watches for film launches. For example, a few years ago Jaeger-LeCoultre made a special reverso watch model with the Batman logo enamelled onto the back of the case for the latest Batman film. These have also now become collector's pieces.

• *The Tudor chronograph has become more and more popular as the Rolex chronograph is not easily available.*

• *The Rolex watch is very strong and well-built, and, even with an example in such a poor condition as the one shown above, can be brought back to new, at a price.*

• *The unusual examples with company logos on them are worth collecting. They provide another unique area as the watches are quite different to the standard models.*

• *Tudor watches have also been produced with quartz movements. These have limited appeal because mechanical examples are always more collectable.*

Where to Buy and See

When starting to collect it is important to go to established dealers and shops (ensure they are members of BADA, LAPADA, the British Horological Institute, or NAADA in the USA), major city and provincial auction houses and any other outlet where you will be given a written full receipt, ideally with a condition report, so that if the watch proves not to be as stated it can easily be returned. Remember there is usually a difference between auction and retail/insurance values.

Auction Houses

Antiquorum Geneva
2 rue de Mont-Blanc
CH-1201 Geneva
Switzerland
Tel: 0041 22 909 2850
www.antiquorum.com

Antiquorum New York
Suite 503
609 Fifth Avenue
New York
NY 10017
USA
Tel: 001 212 750 1103
www.antiquorum.com

Bonhams
101 New Bond Street
London W1Y 0AS
Tel: 0044 20 7393 3900
www.bonhams.com

Christie's
8 King Street, St James
London SW1Y 6QT
Tel: 0044 20 7839 9060
www.christies.com

Christie's South Kensington
85 Old Brompton Road
London SW7 3LD
Tel: 0044 20 7930 6074
www.christies.com

Sotheby's
34–35 New Bond Street
London W1A 2AA
Tel: 0044 20 7293 5000

Useful Websites

www.ebay.com
www.vintageheuer.com
www.nawcc.org
www.preciouswatches.com

Dealers

Anthony Green Antiques
Vault 54
The London Silver Vaults
Chancery House
Chancery Lane
London WC2A 1QS
Tel: 0044 20 7430 0038
www.anthonygreen.com

Graus Antiques
Bond Street Silver Galleries
111–112 New Bond Street
London W1Y 0BQ
Tel: 0044 20 7629 6680
(Mainly bejewelled watches)

Harper of York
2–4 Munster Gate
York
North Yorkshire Y01 7HL
Tel: 0044 1904 632634

Johnny Wachsmann
Pieces of Time
Unit 17–19
1–7 Davies Mews
London W1Y 2LP
Tel: 0044 20 7629 2422/
0044 20 7629 3272
www.antique-watch.com

Marcus
170 Old Bond Street
London W???
Tel: 0044 20 7290 6500

Ogden of Harrogate Ltd
38 James Street
Harrogate
North Yorkshire
Tel: 01423 504123

Somlo Antiques
7 Piccadilly Arcade,
London SW1Y 6NH
Tel: 020 7499 6526
www.somlo.com

Tourneau
500 Madison Avenue
New York
NY 10022
USA
Tel: 001 212 758 6098
(Branches across the USA)

Watch Gallery
129 Fulham Road
London SW5
Tel: 0044 20 7581 3239

Wempe
700 Fifth Avenue
New York
NY 10019
USA
Tel: 001 212 397 9000

Fairs

Brunel Clock & Watch Fair
PO Box 273
Uxbridge
Middlesex UB9 4LP
Tel: 0044 1895 834694/
0044 1895 834357
Fax: 0044 1895 832329/
0044 1895 832904
(Held at Brunel
University, Middlesex)

Clock & Watch Dealers' Fairs
PO Box 54
Oswestry
Shropshire SY10 9WH
Tel: 0044 1691 831162
(Held at Haydock Park
Racecourse, nr Newark)

Midland Clock & Watch Fair
PO Box 273
Uxbridge
Middlesex UB9 4LP
Tel: 0044 1895 834694/
0044 1895 834357
(Held at the National
Motorcycle Museum)

Southampton Watch
& Clock Fair
Sea-Land Services
Unit 202
Solent Business Centre
Millbrook Road West
Southampton SO15 0HW
Tel: 0044 23 8077 0222
(Held at the University
of Southampton)

Associations

Art and Antiques Dealers
League of America
1040 Madison Avenue
New York
NY 10021
Tel: 001 212 772 7197
www.artantiquedealers
league.com

The Antiquarian
Horological Society
New House
High Street
Ticehurst
Sussex TN5 7AL
Tel: 01580 200155

BADA
20 Rutland Gate
London SW7 1BD
Tel: 0044 20 7589 4128
www.bada.org

British Horological
Institute (BHI)
Upton Hall
Upton
Newark
Nottinghamshire
NG23 5TE
Tel: 01636 813795
www.bhi.co.uk

International Watch
& Jewelry Guild
5901 Wesheimer
Suite Z
Houston
TX 77057
Tel: 001 713 783 8188
www.iwjg.com

LAPADA
535 Kings Road
Chelsea
London SW10 0SZ
Tel: 0044 20 7823 3511
www.lapada.co.uk

The National Antique &
Art Dealers Association
of America Inc
220 East 57th Street
New York
NY 10022
Tel: 001 212 826 9707
www.naadaa.org

NAWCC Inc
514 Poplar Street
Columbia
PA 17512-2130
USA
Tel: (001) 717-684-8261
www.nawcc.org

Museums

British Horological
Institute
Upton Hall
Upton
Newark
Nottinghamshire
NG23 5TE
Tel: 0044 1636 813795
www.bhi.co.uk

British Museum
Great Russell Street
London WC1B 3DG
Tel: 0044 20 7323 8000
www.thebritishmuseum.
ac.uk
(Wristwatches are in the
Reserve Collection, viewed
by appointment only)

Le Musée de la Montre
5 Rue Pierre Berçot
Villers Le Lac - Saut
du Doubs
25130 France
Tel: 0033 381 680800
http:montres.fc-net.fr

Musée de l'Horlogerie
et de l'Emaillerie
Route de Malagnou 15
1208 Geneva
Switzerland
Tel: 0041 22 418 6470
http://mah.ville-ge.ch

Musée d'Horlogerie
Château des Monts
Rue des Monis 65
CH2400 Le Locle,
Switzerland
Tel: 0041 32 931 1680
www.manuelebiner.com

Musèe International
d'Horlogerie
Rue des Musées 29,
CH-2301 La Chaux-
de-Fonds
Switzerland
Tel: 0041 32 967 6861
www.mih.ch

National Maritime
Museum
Old Observatory
Greenwich
London SE10 9NF
Tel: 0044 20 8312 6565
www.nmm.ac.uk
(Very small collection)

NAWCC Museum
514 Poplar Street,
Columbia,
PA 17512-2130
USA
Tel: 001 717 684 8261
www.nawcc.org

Science Museum
Exhibition Road
London SW7 2DD
Tel: 0870 870 4868
www.sciencemuseum.
org.uk

Worshipful Company of
Clockmakers of London
Guildhall Library
Aldermanbury
London EC2P 2EJ
www.clockmakers.org

(Remember that many of
the Swiss manufacturers
have their own museums)

Bookshops

G.K. Hadfield
Beck Bank
Great Salkeld
Penrith
Cumbria CA11 9LN
Tel: 0044 1768 870111
www.gkhadfield-tilly.co.uk

Jeffrey Formby Antiques
Orchard Cottage
East Street
Moreton-in-Marsh,
Gloucestershire GL56 0LQ
Tel: 0044 1608 650558
www.formby-clocks.co.uk

Rita Shenton Books
142 Percy Road
Twickenham
TW2 6JG
Tel: 0044 20 8894 6888
www.shentonbooks.com

Repairs &
Restoration

J. Veale
Email:
jerryveale@tiscali.co.uk

Glossary

analogue Indication of time by hands on a watch dial.

anti-magnetic Describes a mechanical wristwatch that is protected from magnetism. Quartz watches usually do not need anti-magnetic protection.

applied numerals Raised metal batons or numbers that are pegged or stuck to the dial.

automatic Watch wound by the movements of the wearer.

automaton watch Watch (usually a repeater) with figures or other devices that move.

back plate The plate that is furthest from the dial and forms the base of the movement.

balance Wheel that controls the going of a watch.

balance spring Spiral spring that regulates timekeeping.

balance staff Arbor to which inner end of balance spring is attached.

barrel Barrel-shaped box that houses the mainspring.

baton numeral Non-numerical form of marker that is used to denote seconds, minutes, and hours.

bezel Rim that holds the watch glass.

bridge Metal plates that secure jewels and pivots in the movement.

bubble back Term used to describe the deeply curved backs of some watch cases.

calendar Feature that indicates the day/date/year.

calibre Specification of the type and size of the watch.

centre seconds Seconds hand central to the main dial; often pivoted with the hour and minute hands at the centre.

champlevé enamel Decoration in which an area of metal is hollowed out and filled with enamel.

chapter ring Ring marked with hours, minutes, or half/quarter-hours.

cabochon Term to describe the uncut stone that is found in some winding crowns.

carat (ct) Also spelt karat. Pure gold is 24ct but is too soft to be used for watch cases. Therefore an alloy of gold and other metals is used – 18ct, for example, indicates that while 18 parts are gold the remaining six are other metals.

chronograph Watch with a centre seconds hand that f unctions as a stopwatch.

chronometer Watch with a detent escapement; also the Swiss term for a very accurate movement.

cloisonné Decoration in which the enamel is fired in cloisons (or compartments) outlined in flat metal wire.

compensation balance Balance that compensates for changes in temperature.

complication Term used to describe a mechanical wristwatch that has more than one function.

crown Also known as a winding crown, this knob, usually at 3 o'clock, is used for winding the movement, setting the hands, and the date.

crystal A name for the cover over the dial of the wristwatch. It can also be referred to as a glass, which is the material these covers were once made of – nowadays they are more commonly made from plastic or synthetic sapphire.

date aperture Small opening on dial through which date is displayed.

dial Name for the watch face that shows hours, minutes, and seconds.

digital dial Dial without hands on which hours and minutes are instead shown by numerals.

ébauche Rough or partly finished movements.

engine turning Decorative, textured patterns created by turning metal on an machine-driven lathe.

escapement Part of the movement that controls the driving power and gives impulse to the balance.

escape wheel This is the last wheel in the going train, which gives impulse to the balance and controls the watch's rate with a pallet fork.

flyback hand Hand that "flies" back to zero or to join another hand.

form watch Watch with a case that resembles another object.

frame The pillars and plates of a movement.

frequency Refers both to the number of vibrations per hour in a mechanical watch and oscillations per second of a quartz movement.

going barrel Barrel, with wheel on outer edge, containing mainspring.

guilloche Pattern created in the form of concentric waves, often used as decoration on watch dials to give them a watered-silk appearance.

hairspring Common name for the balance spring.

half-hunter case Case with a central aperture in the front lid to show the dial and hands.

helical hairspring Balance spring formed into a helix, often used with chronometer or detent escapements.

Hertz (Hz) The number of oscillations per second of electronic watches.

incabloc A brand name shock absorber for a watch's movement.

jacquemart (or jack) Figure or automaton that strikes the bell on repeater watches.

jewelled Movement bearings of precious or semi-precious stone used to reduce friction.

LCD Liquid crystal display, continuously shows time in quartz watches.

LED Stands for light-emitting diode, which shows the time in electric watches but must be operated by a push button.

lever Escapement in which the impulse is transmitted by a lever.

ligne Term used to describe the size of a movement. One ligne is 2.256mm or 1/12th of a French foot.

lugs Part of wristwatch to which strap is attached.

mainspring Spring that provides the driving power for the watch.

maintaining power Device for driving a watch movement that would otherwise stop when it was being wound.

minute repeater A wristwatch that can sound the hours, quarters, and minutes when the relevant button or slide is pressed.

moonphase A watch that shows the relevant moon phases through an aperture on the dial face.

motion work Wheels and pinions beneath the dial that drive the hands.

oscillation Describes the regular movement of the balance wheel back and forth between two points.

pallet Part or parts of the escapement on which the escape wheel acts.

perpetual calendar Calendar watch that allows for short months and leap years without manual adjustment.

pillars The posts between a movement's plates.

pinion The driven gear, with teeth known as "leaves".

power reserve indicator Subsidiary dial that shows the state of winding.

quartz Watches known as quartz watches employ an electric current that makes a rock crystal oscillate on a constant basis. Most quartz watch movements today have a synthetic crystal.

rattrapanté Term for a split-second function where the hand has a flyback mechanism.

repeater Movement that chimes the time on demand.

rolled gold Heavy gold plate applied to another metal.

rotor Pivoted weight in an automatic watch that winds automatic watches through the wearer's arm movement.

screwback watch Watch with the back screwed down rather than hinged.

screw-down crown Describes when the crown can be screwed tightly into the case to prevent water or dust entering the movement.

self-winding (or perpetual) watch Watch wound by the movements of the wearer.

shock-resistant Watches are shock-resistant if when dropped onto hard wooden surface from a height of 1m (3ft) they do not stop running, and there is no more than a 60-second variation in their daily rate.

skeleton watch Watch where the movement is chiefly visible through the dial, with only the chapter ring retained. The back of the case is often crystal so that the movement can be seen from both sides.

solar-powered Watches that have special light capturing panels that convert the light into an electrical force to drive the quartz movement.

subsidiary dial Small extra dial, often showing seconds, set within the main dial.

Swiss -made Only applicable to a watch in which at least 50 per cent of the parts are made in Switzerland. Their assembly, completion, and testing must also have been carried out there.

tachometer A system for calculating speed and revolutions found on the outer ring of a watch's dial.

tourbillon A revolving cage that holds the movement and prevents positional errors in the the watch's running.

train Wheels and pinions geared to one another, transmits power.

water-resistant Term preferred to waterproof by most wristwatch manufacturers for watches that are able to withstand water pressure for 30 minutes at 1m (3ft) and 90 seconds at 20m (6ft).

world-timer watch Watch that can show the current time in any of the world's time zones.

Bibliography

A selection of books that are still in print or can be obtained secondhand from specialist booksellers (*see* p153).

Balfour, Michael, *The Classic Watch*, Todtri Publications, 2002

Braun, Peter, *Wristwatch Annual 2004*, Abbeville Press, 2003

Brunner, G. L., *Mastering Time, TAG-Heuer*, Editions Assouline, 1997

Brunner, G. L. & Pfeiffer-Belli, C., *Wristwatches*, Konemann, 1999

Brunner, G. L., Pfeiffer-Belli, and Wehrl, M. K., *Audemars Piguet & Co*, Callwey Verlag, 1992

Childers, Caroline, *Designers of Time*, Rizzoli, 1999

Childers, Caroline, *Masters of the Millennium*, Rizzoli, 2000

Childers, Caroline, *Watches 2000*, Rizzoli, 2000

Cologni, F. & Mocchetti, E,, *Made by Cartier: 150 Years of Tradition & Innovation*, Abbeville Press, 1993

Cologni, F. & Flechon, Dominique, *Cartier: the Tank Watch*, Flammarion, 1998

Cologni, Franco et al, *Piaget Watches and Wonders*, Abbeville Press, 1998

Dowling, James, *Rolex Wristwatches*, Schiffer Publishing, 2001

Dowling, James & Hess, Jeffrey P., *The Rolex Wristwatches*, Schiffer Publishing, 1997

Edwards, Frank, *Wristwatches: A Connoisseurís Guide*, Apple Press, 1997

Faber, Edward & Unger, Stewart, *American Wristwatches*, Schiffer Publishing, 1989

Hampel, Heinz, *Automatic Wristwatches from Switzerland*, Schiffer Publishing, 1995

Huber, M., & Banberry, *Patek Philippe Wristwatches*, Patek Philippe, 1998

Kahlert, H., Muhe, R. & Brunner, G., *Wristwatches*, Schiffer Publishing, 1999

Kreuzer, Anton, *Omega Designs*, Schiffer Publishing, 1996

Lambelet, C., & Coen, L., *The World of Vacheron Constantin*, Lausanne Geneva, 1992

Lang, Gerd R. & Meis, Reinhard, *Chronograph Wristwatches*, Schiffer Publishing, 1993

Lhote, Gilles, & Lassaussois, Jean, *The World of Watches*, Greenwich Editions, 1999

Levenberg, Juri, *Russian Wristwatches*, Schiffer Publishing, 1995

Naas, Roberta & Childers, Caroline, *Master Wristwatches*, Rizzoli, 1999

Osterhausen, F. Van, *The Movado History*, Schiffer Publishing, 1996

Pannier, René, *Collectible Wristwatches*, Editions Flammarion, 2001

Richon, M., *Omega Saga*, Fondation Adrien Brandt, 1998

Richter, Benno, *Breitling Timepieces: 1884 to the Present*, Schiffer Publishing, 2000

Rondeau, Renae, *Hamilton Wristwatches: A Collectors Guide*, Schiffer Publishing, 1999

Rondeau, Renae, *The Watch of the Future: the Story of the Hamilton Electric Watch*, Schiffer Publishing, 1999

Selby, Isabella de Lisle, *Wristwatches ID*, Apple Press, 1997

Shugart, Cooksey, Engle, Tom, & Gilbert, Richard E., *Complete Price Guide to Watches*, Cooksey Shugart, 2002

Skeet, Martin & Urul, Nick, *Vintage Rolex Sports Models*, Schiffer Publishing, 2002

Viola, Gerald & Brunner, Gisbert L., *Time in Gold Wristwatches*, Schiffer Publishing, 1988

Zagoory, Jac & Chan, Hilda, *A Time to Watch*, ChiuZac, 1985

Index

Acknowledgments

Mitchell Beazley would like to thank the following for their kind permission to reproduce the photographs in this book:

Key
t top **b** bottom **c** centre **l** left **r** right
OPG Octopus Publishing Group

Front cover: l Patek Philippe; r IWC, International Watch Company, Schaffhausen, Switzerland; Back cover: l Tissot SA; r OPG/Steve Tanner/Jonathan Scatchard.

Alain Silberstein 54 bl;
Bonhams 16, 20 l, 36 tl, 48 tl, 70, 72, 88, 91, 97, 103 t, 106, 107 t, 126, 128, 131 t, 132, 134, 135, 145, 151 b;
Breitling SA 25 tl, tr, 47 t;
Bulova Corporation 48 br;
Cartier 33 br/M Feinberg, 51 br/C Cournet, 52 r/G Panséri, 54 tl/L Hamani, 57 l & r/M Feinberg;
Christie's Images 10 l, 33 tl, 40 l, 45 br, 62, 74, 118, 119, 140, 141 tl, tr, b/Live And Let Die © 1973 Danjaq, LLC And United Artists Corporation. All Rights Reserved. Courtesy of MGM CLIP+STILL, 144, 148, 149 t, b, 151 t;
Collection of Musée international d'horlogerie, La Chaux-de-Fonds-Suisse 28 r;
Eterna SA 42 tr, 64, 96;
Franck Muller 52 c;
Frédérique Crestin-Billet 108;
Frederique Constant SA 82;
Hamilton Watch Co Ltd 8, 11 bl, 34 c, 36 bl, 45 tr, 56, 78, 100, 104, 105 t, bl, br;
IWC, International Watch Company, Schaffhausen, Switzerland 9, 19 tr, 22 tl, tcl, tcr, tr, bl, br, 42 tl, 55, 66, 67 t, b, 79, 93, 99 b, 120, 121 l, r;
Jaeger-LeCoultre SA 27, 85 l, r, 89;

Montres Breguet SA 76, 77, 83 bl, br;
Montres Corum (UK) Ltd 109 t;
Movado Group, Inc 31 r, 99 t;
Officine Panerai 52 l;
OMEGA SA 7, 11 tr, 29 b, 30 tl, 30 br, 33 bl, 35 b, 38 l, 40 c, 42 bl, 45 tl, bl, 46 r, 48 bl, 49 r, 50 t, bl, 51 tr, 73 t, bl, br, 80, 83 t, 84 l, r, 101 t, b, 111, 122, 123 l, r, 124, 125 t, b, 127, 129;
OPG/Steve Tanner 11 tl, 13 l, 15 t, b, 24 b, 28 l, 31 l, 33 tr, 39 tr, 138;
OPG/Steve Tanner/Andrew Hilliard 20 r, 21 tr;
OPG/Steve Tanner/Nick Jenkins 113;
OPG/Steve Tanner/Jonathan Scatchard 1, 3 l, r, 19 tl, 29 t, 32 tl, tr, 35 c, 38 r, 41 tl, tr, br, 44 t, c, b, 47 bl, 112;
OPG/Steve Tanner/Private Collection 18 b, 20 cl, cr, 21 tl, tc, cl, c, cr, bl, br, 150 l, r;
OPG/Miller's Collectables/Robin Saker 13 r, 14 tl, tr, bl, 28 c, 34 r, 36 br, 40 r, 43 l, r, 46 l, 58, 60, 61, 63, 90;
Orbita Corporation 19 b;
Parmigiani Fleurier 107 b/10 days power reserve/Bugatti model;
Patek Philippe 39 bl, 65 tl, tr, b, 75 t, b, 86, 87, 116, 117;
Piaget 109 b;
Rado Watch Company Ltd 51 tl;
Seiko UK Ltd 102;
Sotheby's 12 r, 25 b, 30 tr, bl, 36 tr, 37, 39 tl, 39 br, 42 br, 59, 68, 69, 81 cr, bl, br, 98, 110, 139 l, r, 142, 143, 146, 147;
The Swatch Group Ltd 10 r, 114;
TAG Heuer SA 11 br, 12 l, 14 br, 34 l, 49 l, 51 bl, 103 b, 130, 131 b, 133 t, b, 136 l, r, 137 l, r;
Tissot SA 24 t, br, 32 b, 35 t, 38 c, 41 bl, 47 br, 50 br, 53 t, b, 54 tr, 92, 115;
Uylsse Nardin 54 br, 81 tl, tr, 94, 95;
Zenith 48 tr, 71 t, b.